Caring for Your Aging Parents

When Love Is Not Enough

Barbara Deane

NAVPRESS

A MINISTRY OF THE NAVIGATORS
P.O. BOX 6000, COLORADO SPRINGS, COLORADO 80934

The Navigators is an international Christian organization. Jesus Christ gave His followers the Great Commission to go and make disciples (Matthew 28:19). The aim of The Navigators is to help fulfill that commission by multiplying laborers for Christ in every nation.

NavPress is the publishing ministry of The Navigators. NavPress publications are tools to help Christians grow. Although publications alone cannot make disciples or change lives, they can help believers learn biblical discipleship, and apply what they learn to their lives and ministries.

Second printing, 1990

Excerpts from "Why Can't I Forgive?" by David W. Brewer, *Discipleship Journal*, Issue 46, 1988, are reprented with permission from the author. "The Gift of Dependency" by Peggy Harrar, *Change*, the newsletter of the National Support Center for Families of the Aging, Swarthmore, PA: Summer 1984, No. 3, is used with permission of the author. "Personal Record File" reprinted from *Estates: Planning Ahead* (a personal manual for estate planning) by Pamela Priest Naeve and Isabel Walker, with the permission of the publisher, the northern California Cancer Program, 1301 Shoreway Rd., Ste. 425, Belmont CA 94002.

Scripture quotations in this publication are from the *Holy Bible: New International Version* (NIV). Copyright © 1973, 1978, 1984, International Bible Society. Used by permission of Zondervan Bible Publishers. Other versions used include: the *Revised Standard Version Bible* (RSV), copyright 1946, 1952, 1971, by the Divison of Christian Education of the National Council of the Churches of Christ in the USA, used by permission, all rights reserved; the *Good News Bible: Today's English Version* (TEV), copyright © American Bible Society 1966, 1971, 1976; and the *King James Version* (KJV).

Printed in the United States of America

Contents

*This book is dedicated
to the members of
Christian Caregivers Support Group.
This is your book;
your love and caring
have made it possible.*

Author

Barbara Deane has been a freelance writer for local and national magazines for over fifteen years. A member of the American Society of Journalists and Authors, her work has appeared in *Ladies' Home Journal, Woman's Day, Family Circle, Parenting, Reader's Digest, Virtue,* and many other secular and religious publications. She has been a college English teacher, taught creative writing and adult education classes, and an active Sunday school teacher and seminar leader. For eight years (1978 to 1986), she took care of her elderly mother in her home, and in 1984, she co-founded Christian Caregivers, a support group for those caring for ill or frail elderly family members. She continues to co-lead Christian Caregivers and is active in community educational activities on issues of aging and caregiving.

Acknowledgments

So many people have taught me about the needs of elderly parents and how to be a better caregiver. This book could not have been written without them. I'd like to gratefully acknowledge the help and encouragement of

Helen Hight, Joyce Terry, R.N., Rev. Ned Holmgren, Dennis Stone, M.D., Victoria Schlintz, R.N., Jane Dewey Heald, M.S., Mary Thorman, M.S.W., Lori Cutler, Ph.D., Pris Tudor, M.S.W., Linda Fodrini-Johnson, M.S.W., Rose Swanson, Jean Hinckley, Lois-Lyn Hardy-Smith, Ph.D., Rev. David Jobe, Bonnie Kick, R.N., Robert Brindley, Pharm.D., Leslie Dahm, Maureen Rafferty, LaRue Boswell, Margaret Anderson, Margaret Carr, Glenn Corlew, Ruth Fischer, Neita Harkins, Judy Hungerford, Margaret Murray, Alyce Nolte, Geneva Parrish, Gregory Phillips, M.S.W., Jean Marana, M.S.W., Bob Reiley, Lee Senst, Helena Veen, Ruth Walden, the late Alice Torano, Kathy Wisner, Sunny Urricelqui, Bud McCrae, Dr. James Seeber, Doris Larsen, Vicki Harrington, R.N., Peg Happersett, Caroline Leslie, R.N., Liz Rummel, Robert Lauderdale, Nancy Kinrade, R.N., Carol Cole Collins, M.A. M.F.C.C., Robert and Enid Tatje, Liz Wright and the staff and volunteers of Diablo Valley Foundation for the Aging, and many others, especially my husband, Douglas Deane, and my late parents, Raymond and Mary Elizabeth Knorr.

As Christians Care for Elderly Parents

I was a caregiver for my parents for years before the word *caregiver* was even in my vocabulary. But in 1984 I learned that I was part of "the sandwich generation"—middle-aged people, mostly women, who take care of both old and young. We are the generation in the middle.

Families have been taking care of their elderly throughout the ages. What is new is the large number of elderly people who need care. The fastest-growing segment of the U.S. population is the group over eighty-five. As their numbers continue to grow, the number of caregivers grows with them.

An estimated seven million Americans now care for an elderly parent in the home. But *caregiver* is a broad term that includes much more than home care. Long before my widowed mother came to live with me, I helped her and my father to live independently. And even if a parent has to be placed in a board-and-care home or nursing home, care by the family continues. If the people giving this type of non-live-in care were included in the figures, the number of caregivers would be much greater.

So, if you have joined the ranks of caregivers, the first thing you must realize is that you are not alone. This is important. You may feel isolated with your new responsibilities. You may even be in shock.

It's a shock to discover that your parents are no longer strong enough to take care of all their own needs. It also comes as a shock when you find that caregiving is much more difficult than you'd realized. As a friend once said, "Nobody trained us for this!" Accompanying the shock of unfamiliar responsibilities is the emotional shock. Watching your loved ones decline in health and strength is painful. Caregiving is painful. Nobody ever tells you that.

"I don't mind the physical and financial responsibilities. I think I could handle them," said one caregiver. "But nobody ever told me about being unable to comfort my mother's anxieties and fears in her old age. This is the ache that never goes away."

It's also a shock when Christians who are caring for the elderly realize that their family and friends (even Christian friends in the church) don't understand what they're going through. Most people are just not comfortable talking about old age and death. Who, then, can caregivers talk to?

I faced this problem in 1984. I had been caring for my mother in my home for six years when I received an assignment from *Ladies' Home Journal* to write an article on problems faced by sandwich generation people caring for the elderly (published as "When Elderly Parents Need Help" in March, 1985). Interviewing experts in the field and other caregivers was truly a revelation. For the first time, I realized that many of the experiences I had thought were mine alone were actually commonplace. I learned that emotions I had condemned myself for feeling were actually normal. My problem was not that I had these emotions—they were to be expected—but the way I was handling them.

These may be the very same emotions that you are experiencing as a caregiver today. You may feel deeply discouraged, lonely, isolated, misunderstood, and friendless. You may have deep-seated feelings of guilt and anger. Your self-esteem may be at an all-time low. There's no prestige in this role. Nobody hands you any bouquets. Even the person receiving your care may not appreciate what you're doing—you may be just one more reminder of his or her growing helplessness and dependency.

At just such a low point in my own caregiving experience, I interviewed the Rev. Ned Holmgren, a Christian marriage and family counselor, for my article. Through him I met Helen Hight, who was caring for her mother, confined to a wheelchair by arthritis, in Helen's home. For some time, she'd wanted to start a Christian support group for caregivers, to create a safe place for us to talk about our feelings, to pray for and with each other, and to give each other information, encouragement, and affirmation as persons. We could not and would not solve all our problems but God would be our most important resource and Jesus our Master Caregiver.

So we stepped out in faith and started Christian Caregivers, knowing that there was a need and trusting God to meet it. That He did, beyond our wildest dreams. As a group, Christian Caregivers became a channel through which God's love and caring have reached many people. Although each of us individually was doing God's will, together we were better able to, in Helen's words, "become a suit of clothes that the Holy Spirit wears." We were no longer alone.

It's tempting, as a solitary caregiver, to begin to believe that God has abandoned you. I now know that when I felt most abandoned and alone, God, by sending my mother to live with us, was actually putting me through *His* school in my own home to teach me about old age in the most effective way possible: *through experience.* I can look back now and see that so many things that I found difficult and even distasteful were filled with His grace.

One reason for writing this book is to give you hope and to encourage you to see caregiving as an opportunity sent by God for your own spiritual growth and maturity. It isn't easy, but then, anything that matures us as Christians is never easy. Caregiving will stretch you and try you, probably more than anything you've ever done before.

Yet it shouldn't be necessary for you to go through this alone. God has promised to be with us always, and He is providing answers to caregivers' cries for help. I hope that this book will be one of those answers.

I have tried to write the book that I wish I had when I started helping my parents. Its perspective is my own experience and pain; nearly every mistake mentioned in this book is one that I made myself at one time or another. In addition, many other caregivers have been willing to share their stories with me. Except when noted, names have been changed and details altered in order to protect their privacy.

Although you will find information in this book, to inform is not its primary purpose. You will not learn here, for example, how to transfer a patient from bed to wheelchair. In the Appendix, I refer to other sources for this type of instruction.

In the first six chapters, the emphasis is on your emotional and spiritual needs and how they intertwine with the needs of the person you are caring for and with those of other family members. These chapters deal with love and healing, honest communications, understanding, and forgiveness. Chapter 7 is transitional. In talking about money within families, it's important not to mix emotional needs with practical needs. (Before you make any decisions or take any action based on the content of this chapter, consult an accountant or a lawyer.) Chapters 8 through 11 are more practical. If you are currently experiencing a housing, medical, or legal crisis or don't know where to turn for help for an immediate problem, you may want to go immediately to this part of the book. Chapter 12, "Walking Through the Valley of the Shadow of Death," brings you full circle back to your emotional needs when helping a dying parent.

Nothing in your situation may change as a result of reading this book. But, as you allow God to work in your life, you will change, and that will make all the difference. When relationships—especially the relationship between yourself and God—are sound, practical problems become easier to deal with. When they are not, caregiving becomes difficult and sometimes impossible. Caring for elderly parents can be filled with sorrow, and it can be filled with joy. Often, the joy comes mixed in the same cup with the sorrow. Yet the cup we drink willingly from His hand is never without its blessing. That this book may be a part of that blessing is my prayer for you.

Note: Pronouns are a perennial problem in the English language. "He or she" is awkward and wordy. So, since most caregivers and a majority of the elderly are women, I often refer to them as "she," except where the specific person being referred to is obviously male. I sincerely hope that nobody feels excluded by my choice of pronouns.

1

The Crucible of Caring

*"When you pass through deep
waters, I will be with you; your
troubles will not overwhelm you.
When you pass through fire, you
will not be burned; the hard trials
that come will not hurt you."*
Isaiah 43:2, TEV

I s caregiving "walking through the fire"? For many caregivers it is. Who are the millions of people going through the trials of caregiving?

Statisticians tell us that a typical caregiver is a woman in her fifties. But caregivers are actually very diverse. You may be in your late thirties or early forties, the last-born child of an older mother. You may be an "empty nester" or you may have children at home. You may never have married, or be divorced or widowed. Either you or your spouse may be retired. You may be as old as seventy-five, taking care of a parent in his or her nineties. You may be male. You may be a grandson or granddaughter. You may be rich, poor, or in-between.

You may have volunteered for caregiving or been selected, either willingly or unwillingly, by your parent or siblings. You may have "fallen into" the job only because you're the child living closest to your parents.

No matter who you are or how you got there, the one thing that caregivers seem to have in common is stress. Often, this is because they're exhausted. At various times, they're called upon to

▶ Take their parent shopping or shop for her, buying food, clothing, medicine, and other necessities.
▶ Chauffeur parent to the doctor and appointments.
▶ Supervise or actually take over the parent's finances. Pay bills, balance checkbooks, and act as trustee if large sums of money are concerned. Plan for the wisest use of available financial resources for future care.
▶ Deal with the various bureaucracies that aid the elderly—e.g., Social Security, Medicare, and private health insurance. Know what the parent is eligible to receive, fill out forms, submit claims, and monitor payments.
▶ Hire and supervise housekeeping, health care, and other help that comes into the home (or do it themselves).

▶Supervise or personally take care of the parent's physical needs, such as meals (including special diets), exercise, sleep, bathing, toileting, hairwashing, toenail cutting, etc.

▶Supervise the parent's medical care. Deal with doctors, nurses, and home health aides, and supervise medications. Adapt a home to the needs of someone with the chronic illnesses and sensory deprivations of old age.

▶Make provisions for meeting the parent's social needs. Try to arrange visits and outings and find companionship for her (or become the companion themselves).

▶Give emotional and spiritual support.

Are you exhausted from simply reading this list? If you are doing all of the above, you are probably not giving yourself nearly enough credit. If you are not yet doing it, you're probably thinking, "I don't know how to do these things." As one Christian Caregiver said at a support group meeting, "Nobody ever trained me for this!"

Exactly. There's a lot to learn, yet somehow caregivers are supposed to be instant experts on the legal and medical aspects of aging and also know how to give intense personal care while at the same time caring for their own families and/ or holding down jobs outside the home. No wonder so many of them burn out.

If they try to do this without help, they are attempting the impossible. At the same time, they may be setting themselves up for great emotional damage.

"I will make my parents happy," they think. "I will make things better." Instead, things get worse. When caregivers fail, as they must, they feel terrible about themselves. Sometimes they become angry with God. "God didn't do what I wanted Him to do. What did I do wrong?" they say.

Do you recognize yourself in this description? You must realize that no matter how hard you work, your parent is not going to get better. There may be some temporary improvements, but eventually everybody dies. Christians, of all people, should not see death as failure. Yet too often they do.

You also must realize that, over time, your parent's needs will increase while the amount of time and energy you have to give them will remain the same. This can lead to deep discouragement. The feeling that whatever you do is never enough is painful. But the pain you feel is not the last word on the subject. God has the last word: "When you pass through deep waters, I will be with you; your troubles will not overwhelm you" (Isaiah 43:2, TEV). Do you believe that, even though you may be feeling overwhelmed? Do you believe God or your feelings?

THE SPIRITUAL BENEFITS OF CAREGIVING

Nobody likes to be hurt, and nobody really believes anyone who says, "Trust me. This is painful, but it will be good for you." I would not dare to say this except that God has said it first. If you're now walking through His fire, it's a refiner's fire meant to purify you (Malachi 3:2).

What are the benefits He intends to bring you in the caregiving experience?

▶A closer relationship with Him, achieved through trusting.
▶A more mature faith, purified by testing.
▶The ability to face and deal with your negative emotions, such as anger, resentment, guilt, fear, anxiety, sadness, etc., instead of running from them.
▶Healing of your past hurts (and even the healing of entire families).

WHO CONTROLS YOUR LIFE?

Right now, the most important questions in your life are: "Can I really trust God to do all this? Really trust Him?

Trust Him enough to let Him control me during the caregiving experience?"

Many Christians think they are already controlled by God. But they find, when they begin giving care to parents, that they are being controlled by many other forces. Your parents may be controlling you by making you feel guilty if you don't please them. Immature and inappropriate ideas from your early religious training may be controlling you. Society's expectations of what "a good son" or "a good daughter" should do may be controlling you. NonChristians may be controlling you; you may be performing for their benefit in order to be a "good witness."

You may think your parent or siblings who won't help are the problem, but your real problem is almost always yourself. Can you trust God enough to give up these other sources of control and be controlled by Him alone? You may receive a great deal of approval from these other sources of control. Letting God have control may be a tremendous struggle. But it's worth the effort, because if you are controlled by anybody or anything other than God, you will be miserable. He may, even now, be using your distress to draw you to Him.

But to get out from under these controlling forces that are not of God, you have to recognize them. The following examples may help you to analyze your own reactions. Who or what is controlling you right now?

Control by the Culture: Denial

In the early stages of caregiving, both parent and adult child tend to deny what's really going on. In our culture, aging is bad, dependence is taboo, and any sign that this may be happening arouses great anxiety. The care of elderly relatives forces you to face things you'd rather not face and think about things you'd rather not think about, such as your own death. Denial is nature's way of protecting you from whatever you find too threatening.

Fear of aging is deeply ingrained in our culture. We tend to think aging happens to other people, but not to me nor to my loved one. But it does, and outsiders will usually see it before we do.

What can you do if you see what's happening but your parent refuses to admit it? Perhaps nothing if your parent is really stubborn. Your parent's denial will usually end with a crisis, such as a fall or an illness; then it's no longer possible to keep up the pretense that all is well.

Denial by caregivers can also be caused by fear of their own emotions or of others' disapproval. They think, "I could never put my mother in a nursing home. It would make me feel too guilty." This attitude can be dangerous if it puts the elder at risk.

Alma had been warned by her mother's doctor that her mother, who had Alzheimer's disease, was no longer capable of living alone. But Alma couldn't bear to end her mother's independence. So she denied that her mother was really "that bad." The doctor was exaggerating.

One day, an out-of-work youth on drugs followed Alma's mother home from a convenience store. Her mother was no longer capable of realizing that it was not safe to let him in. She opened the door and he beat and robbed her. Alma thought she had been acting out of love for her mother, but she was really being controlled by her own emotions. Our culture doesn't approve of putting parents in nursing homes; if you do, you're going to feel bad about yourself. So Alma felt good about herself—until her mother got hurt. Then she paid a terrible price in guilt for her self-delusion.

Control by False Guilt: The Compassion Trap

Sometimes, what caregivers call "guilt" may actually be sadness about not being able to do what they would like to do for an elderly loved one. They won't be able to "fix" old age no matter how hard they try. This causes deep distress, which is sometimes mistaken for guilt.

Sometimes caregivers (who tend to be giving, loving people—that's why they're caregivers) fall into the trap of over-identifying with the person receiving care. Their feelings of deep compassion cause them to feel everything their loved one is feeling to the point where they almost lose their own identity. It may be similar to the "survivor's guilt" that's sometimes experienced after a disaster: "Why am I still alive when they're all dead?"

A caregiver begins to feel guilty because she can enjoy life while her frail, elderly parent is confined by his disabilities to one room. She may begin to stay home because going out under these circumstances makes her feel guilty. This distress may also be a way of saying, "My parent shouldn't be like this. This shouldn't be happening to him."

But each person ages in his own way and in his own time, and not according to the caregiver's (or anybody else's) blueprint. Now is your parent's time to grow old and die, not yours. Even if you would like to, you can't share this experience.

Trying to share it is not healthy caregiving. You are not required to suffer somebody else's pain for him. "Bear one another's burdens and so fulfill the law of Christ" (Galatians 6:3, RSV) is frequently taken out of context and applied unconditionally. But if you read on, verse 5 says, "But each man will have to bear his own load." Everybody is given his own life to live, and the burdens and sorrows that come with it are his alone. Others can help him, but they can't shoulder his burden along with their own. You can help your parent with the burdens of his old age, but you can't be old for him. There is a difference. Losing sight of this difference leads to inappropriate guilt and then to inappropriate behavior in an effort to avoid the guilt feelings.

Control by the Parent: Guilt
When children are young, they want to win their parents' approval, and parents can easily control children by making them feel guilty if they do anything the parents disapprove of. Mature parents no longer try to control adult children, and mature adult children no longer feel guilty when they don't please their parents. But not everybody is mature. Some elderly parents and adult children make it to the caregiving

stage with this childish pattern of behavior still intact.

Elizabeth and Joe were brought up to "never talk back to your parents." When Joe's father, a retired pastor, moved in with them at the age of eighty-eight, he was still the autocrat of Joe's childhood. Whenever Papa did or said something to upset Elizabeth, Joe told her, "Don't say anything. He'll never change."

This policy left Elizabeth seething with suppressed rage and created unbearable tension in the household. The result of trying to keep the peace in this way was anything but peaceful, because Joe couldn't set reasonable limits on his father's behavior or defend his wife from attack without feeling guilty.

This was a false guilt. Joe was no longer a little child. He was a married man whose first loyalty should have been to his wife. But in relating to his father, he still felt like a little child inside.

To be controlled by God rather than by his parent, Joe will have to learn to stand up to his father and say no. If you have never said no to a parent, this will be difficult. It does not have to be done disrespectfully. Almost always, the parent who is approached firmly but lovingly learns to adjust to the new relationship. But even if she does not, you will be free to do what God wants you to do. And He wants you to grow up.

Control by the Parent: Pleasers

Many people are brought up to be "pleasers." When they're able to please others, they feel good about themselves. There may be nothing wrong with this until they become caregivers. Parents want to be independent, but they need to be helped. When their needs are incompatible with their wants, it becomes a no-win situation for the caregiver who hopes to please them.

Dawn's mother was constantly angry at her, and Dawn was becoming furious. She held down a full-time job and visited her mother in a board-and-care home at least once a week. She also took her mother to the doctor, ran all her errands, and did as much as she could to make her mother's life better.

But the more she did, the less her mother liked it. Nothing Dawn did met with her approval. She even complained about her to the aides in the home!

What Dawn's mother needed was exactly the kind of care she was receiving. But what she wanted was something Dawn could not give her: her health and independence. Dawn was trying to please her mother by constantly trying to meet her demands for more services. This would never work because the demands were a poor substitute for what her mother really wanted. Meanwhile, the constantly escalating demands were a way of keeping Dawn under her control.

The only way to break these chains is to stop trying to please your parent. Like the child controlled by guilt, you must learn to say no. This means that you must also learn to say no to your own desire to feel good by pleasing others. The key is to look to God and not to your parent for approval. The approval of other caregivers who understand can also help you to give up your need for your parent's approval.

This will not be easy, but it can be done. Both Dawn and Joe eventually learned to say no and were freed from their controlling parents. If you recognize yourself in these stories, there's hope for you, too.

Control by Other Christians: Pride

Both Christians and nonChristians seem to have well-defined ideas about what a Christian is "supposed" to do. Living up to this image is one of the greatest burdens that can be put on a caregiver. Polishing this image may eventually keep you too busy to pay attention to what God really wants from you.

Sharon had taken care of her mother, who was confined to a wheelchair, for years in her home. Many people from Sharon's church had told her what an inspiration she was to them. She was becoming increasingly exhausted by the demands of caregiving, but she never complained.

One day, looking and feeling very stressed-out, she went

to a church luncheon, where she happened to sit next to an older visitor from out of town. She began talking to her about taking care of her mother and how tired she was.

"Don't you have any brothers or sisters?" the visitor asked.

"Two brothers, but what could they do?" Sharon replied.

"Have you ever asked them for money so you could hire help?"

"I couldn't do that!" Sharon gasped.

The visitor looked her in the eye and said, "Honey, that's your pride talking. You know pride's a sin, don't you?"

Sharon went home almost in tears. The woman was right! Her brothers were not Christians and she didn't want to tarnish her Christian image by admitting to them that she couldn't handle everything herself. People in church thought she was "Mrs. Perfect," and she wanted to continue to have their good opinion. But all it amounted to was being controlled by her own pride.

There's a happy ending to this story. Sharon prayed about it, eventually swallowed her pride, and asked for help. Now, her witness is stronger than ever because, in admitting she was hurting, she has become "real." Her image of Christian perfection helped nobody. But sharing her struggles honestly with other Christians has helped many people.

Control by Past Hurts—Free by Grace

Many adults have been hurt by their parents when they were children, sometimes when they were too young even to remember what happened. But these hurts continue to influence their behavior; they're still under the control of a past they don't even remember. Other adults have been hurt by parents in ways they remember only too well—by divorce or desertion, by abuse of various kinds, or sometimes by more subtle emotional battering. They may believe they've forgiven their parents, but under the stress of caregiving the old hurt that was only buried and not healed is reopened and hurts as painfully as ever.

In chapter 4, I discuss in more detail how God can heal these hurts. Ironically, one of the ways is the way of relinquishment. Sometimes, when you have given up all hope of getting anything from the parent who has hurt you, God can perform a miracle of healing. That's what happened to Mary Ellen and her father. This is her story:

"I was one of ten children, the youngest of four girls. My father put food on the table and a roof over our heads, but he never gave us any affection or attention, and he was brutal to the boys. My mother died of a heart attack when she was only fifty-one, the same year I got married.

"We saw my father a couple of times a year. Even though I'd forgiven him when I became a Christian fifteen years ago, I still had a hard time being around him. My healing was a slow process, helped along by a number of different people that God had sent into my life. Over the years, I was able to resolve a lot of problems stemming from my childhood, such as my inability to trust and my tendency to withdraw from people.

"My brothers and sisters all suffered too, in different ways. We haven't had much contact over the years. All we learned at home was competitiveness.

"That's how it was until a little over a year ago when my father had a stroke. He recovered, but he was very weak, and he couldn't take care of himself.

"My brother Mike stepped in and moved Dad to a lovely apartment in a retirement center near his home. It was a disaster! Dad wouldn't keep himself clean and turned the place into a pigsty. He also got paranoid about Mike and his wife and made up awful stories about them. Mike was so upset. He'd tried so hard and here was Dad, yelling and screaming at him. Finally, he told the rest of the family, 'I've had it!' He had forty years of anger built up inside him and he couldn't take it anymore.

"The rest of us panicked. We were afraid he might have to come and live with us. Dad was too disruptive—it'd never work. Most of my brothers and sisters flatly refused to have anything to do with him. I got scared and called my older brother Don, who lives in Washington.

"Don is not a Christian, but he's been in therapy and learned to forgive his father, so he was confident he could handle him. He wrote a terrific letter and sent copies to all the family, inviting them to a family meeting at Mike's home. He outlined the situation and told them we were going to make some decisions about Dad's future. He invited Dad, too.

"Don really confronted Dad, right there in front of all of us. About how he wouldn't take baths or change his clothes. I was so embarrassed I didn't know where to look. Dad just ignored him.

"So Don asked us, 'What are you each willing to do?'

"We listed Dad's needs. We decided he couldn't live with any of his children. He'd never cooperated in a home situation before and it wasn't likely he'd start now. And everybody but Mike lived too far away to come in to help him.

"We came up with a plan: we would hire somebody for eight hours per week to help him with personal care. Dad would pay Mike's wife, who'd been cleaning his apartment, to continue. The three children who were willing would call him weekly to check on him. I would take over handling his finances. I'd come over once a month to write checks and see that his bills were paid.

"Don even figured out that it would cost each of us sixty-seven cents a day to take care of our father! Then he circulated another letter to the family, describing the plan. Only those who wanted to would take part and each of us would do only what he wanted to do. He wrote a letter to Dad, enclosing a copy of this letter, and asked for his cooperation.

"Well—I've seen the most dramatic change in my father since this happened. The paranoia is totally gone. I believe it was caused by his fear of my brother. Mike is a harsh, demanding, controlling man—a lot like his father. My father had treated him very badly when he was young, and now he was weak and helpless and Mike was big and strong. If Mike had ever been physical with him, there's nothing my father could have done.

"I think the meeting did it. He had to sit there and listen to what we had to put up with. Dad is an intelligent man and I think he realized, 'I'd better cooperate or they'll put me in a nursing home.'

"Now my father has become a person I've never known before. He has a sense of humor. I can kid around with him. He expresses gratitude to me. He's even phoned me—which he had never done before in my whole life. I enjoy my visits. I take him out to eat. I ask him all kinds of personal questions and he responds. He even calls me 'Honey.'

"It's still not easy for me to show him affection. I always kiss him hello and good-by, but I've never hugged him. I think that'd make him uncomfortable. But I do take his arm when we're walking together and he seems to like that. I never dreamed this would be possible.

"Now I know my healing is complete. I'm no longer this poor little girl whose father didn't love her, which meant, of course, that she must have been unlovable. I'm praying that my brothers and sisters can come to know the Lord and experience some of this too."

None of this would have happened if Mary Ellen had walked into this caregiving situation with any expectations whatsoever of receiving anything from her father. She'd already given him up, mourned the loss of the loving father she'd never had, and was healed of her deep childhood hurt. Then and only then was she free to act toward her father as God wanted her to. She did not feel any coercion or guilt. She was no longer angry and hurt. She allowed God to act in this situation and He did—miraculously, beyond all expectations.

But the struggle during the years that preceded this story is what made it possible. In these struggles, God is refining gold for His Kingdom.

As a caregiver, you will learn a great deal about the needs of the aging, about what to do about medical and legal problems, about nursing home regulations and Medicare forms.

But the most important lessons are the spiritual ones.

There is a great deal to be learned from the elderly. And God will also teach you a great deal about yourself. Even if you don't see the kind of miracle that Mary Ellen has experienced, you will emerge a better and stronger person. Trust God for that!

2

You Can't "Fix" Old Age

"Honor thy father and thy mother."
Exodus 20:12, KJV

"There's nothing we can do."

It's difficult to accept these words. If they come from a doctor, they seem to dash all our hopes. Modern medical science has led Americans to believe that it can "fix" whatever goes wrong. But it can't.

If elderly parents come to you for help, does "honor your father and your mother" mean that you should be able to solve all their problems? Is this what they should expect? Is this what you should expect of yourself? Should you be able to make your parent a contented and happy elderly person?

The answer to all of these questions is no.

Realistically, neither doctors nor caregivers can "fix" old age; it's not at all like a dented fender. When a doctor says, "There's nothing we can do," he really means that there is no cure for this particular ailment. There's always plenty that he can do to make the patient more comfortable. It's called "supportive care." And, while there's nothing you can do to cure your parents of old age or assure their happiness, there is much that you can do in the realm of supportive care, if only you knew how.

You may need to learn new ways of showing honor that are appropriate to this last stage of life—aging is a new experience for both you and your parent.

The process begins with trying to *understand* what your parents are going through. It goes on to *accepting* them as they are now and not as they were in the past. Along the way, you may have to learn to give up your *need to be in control* of their aging.

Aging is their task, not yours. You can't do it for them, and much as you might like to, you can't spare them from the inevitable pain of the struggle. But you can stand with them as they go through it. Your presence says, "I care"; it says, "Your life has meaning and importance"; it says, "I love you; you are not alone." Never underestimate the importance of your just being there with them.

WHAT ARE THE TASKS OF AGING?

You may believe, as I once did, that nothing much happens during old age. But gerontologists tell us that the elderly experience more stresses than any other age group. Physical changes such as failing eyesight may make reading, television watching, or needlework difficult or impossible. Failing hearing can lead to social withdrawal. Failing strength may isolate the older person at home. The loss of a spouse is probably the most devastating stress of all.

Even a seemingly small loss can greatly diminish your parent's independence and feelings of self-worth. When he has to give up driving, how is he going to feel? Stripped of his manhood? No longer a real person? Washed up? Finished?

Adjusting to Losses

One of the major tasks of aging is adjusting to these losses. The companionship of a spouse, old friends, physical strength, independence, health, and finally, even life itself must be relinquished.

The one thing that is not given up until the final breath is the need for love. Often, as the elderly feel their powers slipping, their need for love seems to increase. Even if they never felt particularly close to their children, they may expect them to meet their need for love, and become angry if they don't receive what they expect. Usually, their demands have the effect of driving away the very love they're seeking. Much so-called problem behavior in the elderly is a disguised way of asking for love.

Achieving Integrity

But there is more to old age than adjusting to losses. Contrary to popular belief, old people still have the capacity for growth and change. Rabbi Abraham Heschel wrote: "The years of old age may enable us to attain the high values we failed to sense, the insights we have missed, the wisdom we ignored. They are indeed formative years, rich in possibilities to unlearn the follies of a lifetime, to see through inbred self-deceptions, to deepen understanding and compassion, to widen the horizon of honesty, to refine the sense of fairness."[1]

Erik Erikson, a psychologist who has written extensively about the stages of adult life, sees achieving integrity as the number one task of later life. This is done by a relinquishment of all that has gone before. You give up willingly this life that you cannot keep, yet you feel that your life was worth living.

"Integrity refers, I think, to a kind of emotional closure; one's existence, as one surveys it, seems to have order and meaning. . . . One can discern the shape and outline of what one has been," writes Maggie Scarf in *Unfinished Business*.[2]

What is "closure" but what Jesus said on the cross about His life: "It is finished." The Greek word translated "finished" means not just over but completed. There was nothing more for Him to do. There is a great deal of satisfaction for anyone who can say that about his life, and much disappointment and grief for anyone who doesn't feel completed at the end.

The person who is still growing in old age is well-described in the Bible as being like a great and noble tree:

> The righteous will flourish like palm trees;
>   they will grow like the cedars of Lebanon.
> They are like trees planted in the house of the LORD,
>   that flourish in the Temple of our God,
>   that still bear fruit in old age
>   and are always green and strong.
>   (Psalm 92:12-14, TEV)

We are fortunate if we know people who, despite physical weaknesses, are spiritually green and strong. When you see someone like that, you are seeing a great work of God; He has given these people the grace to do the work of relinquishment well. They truly understand the meaning of "he who would save his life will lose it" (Matthew 10:39, RSV), and "unless a grain of wheat falls into the earth and dies, it remains alone; but if it dies, it bears much fruit" (John 12:24, RSV).

Modeling Love

There is one more task for the older Christian and that is to model love. When a person can no longer do but simply must be, only the essence is left. If that essence is love, then that's all people see. It draws them irresistibly, just as Jesus' presence drew people.

When I think of this kind of irresistible love, I especially remember our old friend Al Felmlee, who lived in Tampa, Florida. Al had suffered from arthritis for most of his life, and the final years before his death were spent almost entirely in a wheelchair. But a smile was always on his face and a blessing was always on his lips. In church, little children fought each other for the privilege of pushing his wheelchair. People came to visit him just to bathe in the reflected glow of God coming from Al. He was truly "green and strong" and bearing "fruit in old age."

It is not possible to model this kind of love if you are still fighting age as an enemy instead of accepting it as the blessing the psalmist describes. Old age is not a disease. Neither is it a problem to be solved. Aging is a stage of life that must be lived. Other cultures understand this better than we do. The old have their place in the family and in society. But in America, self-worth is often measured by how you look—preferably young, blond, and thin—and how much money you have.

Many of the problems that we see in our elders—anger, contempt and hostility toward the young, cantankerousness, denial, and stubbornness—are caused, not by the aging process alone, but by society's obvious disdain for them, which they internalize.

As long as the elderly are shunned and looked down on by society, we will have elders who are depressed about being old. And as long as caregivers share society's views, they will look at their parents' old age as a problem. Only when you learn to see a wrinkled old face as truly beautiful will you see the opportunities as well as the problems of taking care of your parents.

GETTING PAST THE STEREOTYPES

The task of caregiving will be much more difficult for you if you believe society's stereotypes of the elderly. Why, everybody "knows" that old people are unproductive, sexless, irritable, and cantankerous. They can't learn new things because mental ability declines with age. They're good for nothing but living in the past and boring their relatives.

But every one of these stereotypes is wrong. One of the most hopeful findings of recent research is that mental ability does not decline in a healthy older person. Some functions may slow down, but intelligence and the ability to learn remain fairly constant throughout one's lifespan. Many elderly remain sexually active into their seventies and eighties. And not only are all old people not alike, they actually become more unlike with age, more individual and diverse than young people are.

If you as a caregiver believe these stereotypes, you will not be able to help your parents. You may encourage them to "take it easy," and thereby hasten their decline. You may fail to encourage them to develop new interests to replace those they have had to give up. You may believe the doctor when he says it's "old age."

THE "GIFT OF DEPENDENCY"

As a society, Americans have made a fetish of independence. We almost worship it. It's time to ask ourselves whether dependence is really so awful. Consider what one former caregiver, Peggy Harrar, writing in *Change*, the newsletter of the National Support Center for Families of the Aging, calls "The Gift of Dependency":

> My mother died last week. She lived with us for twenty years. After her stroke five years ago, she became increasingly frail. She, who loved to read, could hardly make out sentences in a book. Who loved to

hold long philosophical discussions, could not find the words. Who had learned to paint in her seventies, could not hold a pencil . . . a sad useless end to a rich, vibrant life, you will say.

And yet, Mother was growing right up to the end. She really became a different person in those last five years. She mellowed. She hated her physical limitations, but she learned to accept them in a gracious way. She'd sometimes been proud and rigid, but she became gentle and appreciative. She sometimes hadn't approved of her grandchildren's lifestyles, but she found she could love them just the same. And they loved her and learned from her what courage means.

These past few weeks, I've been able to tell her how much she meant to all of us. She and I have been able to talk more deeply about some things that have been on her mind. . . . I think we've both been preparing, and we've both been leaning on her abiding faith.

As I've talked with people since her death, I've found I had no idea of the impact Mother had on them. There was an outpouring of appreciation from the druggist, the hair dresser, the people at church, the young people! Even her doctor said, "I want you to know I treasure those moments I had with her."

Mother used to ask me, "Why do you think I'm still here?"

"Well, mother," I'd say, ". . . maybe you're here to teach us some things."

Mother did have one last thing to teach us. Her life was an answer to the questions, "What if I have a stroke? What if I become helpless and dependent?"

Mother showed us what you can do with absolutely nothing.[3]

The Biblical Norm: Inter-Dependence
Could it be that God's ways are not our ways, that He has some purpose in allowing dependence in old age? As the Apostle

Paul told the Corinthians, "God chose what is weak in the world to shame the strong. God chose what is low and despised in the world, even things that are not, to bring to nothing things that are" (1 Corinthians 1:27-28, RSV).

The biblical norm for families, which is also the norm for most societies except the most advanced industrial ones like ours, is interdependence between generations. Each generation has something to contribute to the others, each taking and receiving in turn. Each has a secure place with mutual rights and obligations. Parents are to instruct and nurture, and children are to obey and grow in this nurturing environment. Elders, less numerous in those days, were precious repositories of wisdom, handing down the values of the family and the tribe. When they grew old, they were to be cared for.

Family life is not idealized in Bible stories—it was not presented as an earlier version of "The Waltons." Some elders were not wise, some parents were tyrannical, and obviously, some children didn't turn out well. There was sibling rivalry, jealousy (especially with multiple wives!), and hatred between brothers. There was the same manipulation there always has been: Jacob, for example, was rejected by his father and controlled by his mother. But there was a stability and security in the interdependent extended family that most of us no longer have.

However, studies by sociologists have shown that American families are not nearly as independent as the cultural ideal would indicate. A great deal of help is still passed up and down the generations. And, studies have shown, Americans have not abandoned their elderly. When older people need assistance, they usually turn to their families first.

Unfortunately, given our cult of independence, nobody really understands anymore what the roles are supposed to be. How much should you do for your parents? And how can you help them if they won't accept help? There are elders who would literally die—and do—before they'd accept help from their children. Or, if they do accept help, they feel shamed by it—as if they were failures.

It is unlikely that many of us would want to go back to living with three generations under one roof, although some people have done it successfully. But finances are sometimes such that caregivers feel they have no other choice. Then caregiving is made more difficult by the elders' wounded pride.

Avoid Learned Dependence

At the opposite extreme from parents who insist on independence at all costs are those who want you to take over too much of their lives. If that happens, you will quickly learn that there's no tyranny so dreadful as the tyranny of helplessness. You don't want to encourage "learned dependence" by doing too much for your parent.

A widow will sometimes try to transfer her dependence from her husband to her adult children. He formerly balanced her checkbook and told her what to wear and what to cook for dinner, and now she expects a son or daughter to do the same. This is a crucial time in the life of that family. If a son gives in to the temptation to take his father's place, not only will he shoulder responsibility for his mother before it's necessary, but his mother will have lost what may well be her last chance to become an autonomous adult. I've seen amazing growth take place when an adult child insists that his widowed mother take over her own life. If forced to do so, older adults can change and grow—and, yes, even grow up.

ASSESSING THE PARENT'S CAPABILITIES

One caregiver prayed, "Lord, help me to see my mother as You see her." How does God see her mother? Objectively, as she really is now. Caregivers are often too close to the situation and too emotionally involved in it to see clearly. Often, their parents are too.

Ideally, when a parent's failing health or frailty makes some change necessary, all of the family should be involved in the decision-making process. Unless the parent is mentally incompetent, he should be in on all the discussions and the final choice should be his. However, it seldom works out that way in real life. Typically, the parent insists everything is fine while the adult children press for change.

It's sometimes very difficult to know whether Mom can or can't continue where she is. Is she exaggerating her symptoms to get sympathy and attention? Could a medical treatment or piece of equipment turn the situation around so that she can continue to live alone? How can you tell if a problem is being caused by an inevitable decline due to aging or by something else entirely?

For example, mental confusion in elderly people is often caused by some treatable medical condition. If you accept the stereotype that mental decline is inevitable with aging, you will say, "Well, I guess this is it. Mom is getting senile." But there are many other reasons for mental confusion in the elderly. They include the following:

▶ Poor diet. The elderly living alone sometimes don't feel like fixing a meal, so they subsist on tea and toast. In time, inadequate nutrition can lead to a chemical imbalance that affects the brain, and mental confusion and forgetfulness result.

▶ Medication. Some elderly carry around little sacks of different-colored pills from various doctors. They complain about it, but you can tell they're secretly a little proud of how many pills they take. Sometimes I think it's a contest in which the one who dies with the most pills wins. But it's really no joke. The aging liver doesn't detoxify the blood as rapidly as it did when it was younger, so medicines can cause toxicity (poisoning), one of the symptoms of which is mental confusion.

▶ Alcohol. It is estimated that 10 to 15 percent of older Americans abuse alcohol. About two-thirds of this group are alcoholics of long standing, while the remaining one-third become alcoholics when they suffer grief or loss and turn to alcohol to numb the pain.

This is sometimes difficult for families to detect. Also, doctors frequently miss the role alcohol plays in an elderly patient's health problems because they seldom ask about drinking habits. Alcoholism is treatable at any age, and doctors have had some success with anti-depressants in treating elders who react to grief and loss by turning to alcohol.

▶Depression. Mental confusion is a symptom of clinical depression in the older person. Unfortunately, doctors may miss the diagnosis in a confused older person; the symptoms of depression may be quite different from a younger person's. He may dismiss it as "old age."

In chapter 8 I will suggest calling in experts to help you assess your parent's present condition and needs.

EMOTIONAL RESPONSE TO LOSSES

No matter how much support you give, your parent will still suffer in ways that you can do nothing about. Painful emotions often accompany the losses she experiences with aging. These emotions include the following:

Fear and Anxiety

When your strength is failing, it's hard not to be anxious about what new loss tomorrow may bring. Your parent may fear becoming a burden to her children. A widow living by herself for the first time may be afraid to be alone. Living on a small income may make her anxious about finances. She may not admit to fear and anxiety though. It may come out in constant complaining about trifles, hypochondria, phone calls that disrupt your life, or in just plain orneriness.

My friend Sandy's mother was "difficult" after cancer surgery. Her nasty, sarcastic remarks and short temper were hard to bear. After things had settled down, Sandy asked her, "Mom, why were you so mean to me when you came home from the hospital?" Her mother said, "I was afraid."

Anger

It's normal to be angry when something you value is taken away from you. If your parent's independence is taken away, her natural, normal reaction will be anger. Unfortunately, you may be the only target available; she's angry at you because she's dependent on you. It may not be fair, but that's the way it is. She can't tell your father that she's angry at him because he died and left her alone, but she can and will tell you that you did this or that thing wrong.

Sometimes she may become paranoid. The fear, anger, and hostility she can't admit consciously are projected onto others. She'll say that others are "out to get her" or accuse someone (maybe even you) of stealing her things. This is the hardest thing for the caregiver to bear. After all you've done for her, she accuses you of stealing! But getting defensive and angry, or arguing that you didn't steal anything, probably won't stop the accusations. (Paranoia in the elderly can have many causes. It is a condition that almost always calls for medical attention.)

Jealousy

Martha, a caregiver, showed real empathy for her mother when she said, "I sometimes feel jealous of my daughters. They're so young and carefree, and they have so many opportunities that I didn't have when I was their age. I can understand perfectly why my mother sometimes may feel jealous of me. I can still do so much, while she's confined to one or two rooms."

Guilt

Some elderly people feel that their illnesses and frailties are punishments from God. Others feel guilty because they're becoming a burden, or think they are. This isn't a very pleasant feeling for your parent, so he becomes angry. But if he can shift the guilt to your shoulders—"My children don't pay any attention to me" or "You're never there when I need you"— then he can justify some of his anger.

Sadness and Depression

These are normal reactions to loss, from the loss of eyesight to the loss of a spouse. A normal grieving period must be gone through, but if depression persists twelve to eighteen months after the death of a spouse, then the grief may have triggered a deeper depression that may need to be treated medically.

Loneliness

This, like any of the aforementioned emotions, may be presented in the form of physical symptoms. Grace's mother called her several times each day, complaining of various aches and pains: stomachaches, headaches, her feet, her back, and on and on.

One day Grace asked, "Mother, are you lonely?"

When she admitted she was, Grace said, "You can call me whenever you feel lonely and we'll have a nice, long talk."

The constant calling stopped. Grace's mother was using the physical complaints as an excuse to call. Apparently, to her, illness was a more acceptable reason to ask for help than loneliness.

This is not unusual. Many of your parent's negative emotions will not be communicated openly. They come to you in a kind of code. One of the skills that you, as a caregiver, need to learn is how to decode some of these hidden messages. This is discussed in more detail in the next chapter.

LEARN TO ACCEPT THE CHANGES OF AGING

It may be difficult for you to accept the parent you have now because you're longing to have the parent who used to be.

Dorothy, a caregiver in Michigan, said, "I'm always fussing at my father: 'Straighten your leg; wipe your mouth.' When the aide is there he walks and eats okay, and she's not always fussing at him, telling him what to do. Why can't I leave him alone?"

Dorothy's problem is that she can't give up her mental image of her father as he was before the stroke. If only he'd hold his leg straighter, if only he wouldn't dribble food, he'd be like he was before. The aide has no problem because she sees only the elderly man as he is today. She didn't know him "before." Dorothy's nagging is not only useless but frustrating for both of them. He can't be the way she wants him to be. The stroke has made this impossible.

This is a perennial problem for adult children of the elderly. We think, "If only they would show us more love and approval, if only they wouldn't tell the same old boring stories over and over, if only they didn't have such quick tempers."

It's an exercise in futility. Your only hope is to learn to accept your parent as she really is right now. When you accept someone and stop wishing that she were different, she begins to feel more understood and less threatened. She may let down some of her defenses. She may think, "Maybe it's safe to let out some of my real feelings."

Learning to accept our parents as God accepts us has a tremendously healing effect on our relationship with them.

DON'T ARGUE WITH FEELINGS

As you accept your parent, you become better able to accept her feelings. The natural reaction of caregivers is to try to talk a parent out of her feelings. But arguing with feelings never works. Your parent's feelings are seldom under her rational control. She's no more responsible for having them than for developing cataracts, and they won't go away just because you tell them to. However, they may go away if you support her while she struggles with them.

When your parent expresses some of her negative feelings, she's in good company. Do you remember from Scripture what the widowed Naomi said? She had lost a husband and two sons and she was very angry and bitter. "Don't call me Naomi [pleasant]," she said. "Call me Marah [bitter], because Almighty God has made my life bitter. When I left here, I had plenty, but the LORD has brought me back without a thing. Why call me Naomi when the LORD Almighty has condemned me and sent me trouble?" (Ruth 1:20-21, TEV).

The Bible doesn't record any reply to this, but I don't think Ruth said, "Naomi! Don't talk like that!" She stood by and accepted her mother-in-law's natural feelings. Naomi was feeling abandoned. We can see now that God was preparing a way to take care of her; He had not abandoned her. But she had no way of knowing that. To her, at that moment it felt like abandonment.

It isn't pleasant when your parents vent their negative emotions to you, but it is healthy and necessary that they vent them somewhere. If you can accept these negative emotions as natural, without taking responsibility for them (they're not your fault), they may fade away.

If the negative emotions are disguised, it's often helpful to try to get them out in the open. You do this by "active listening," which is explained fully in the next chapter.

When caregivers do not understand the processes of aging or realize the reasons behind their parents' behavior, they feel a great deal of false guilt and unnecessary anger. With a better understanding comes a freedom from guilt—neither the losses that come with age nor the emotional reaction to them are your fault. A better understanding can also free you from some of your anger. Although it may seem like it at times, your parent is not behaving in irritating ways to provoke you.

At any rate, there may be little you can do directly to change the parent's behavior. What you can learn to change is your own reaction to it, and this may require a whole new set of unfamiliar skills.

NOTES: 1. Rabbi Abraham Heschel in testimony given before the White House Conference on Aging in 1961, quoted in Robert N. Butler, M.D., *Why Survive? Being Old in America* (New York: Harper & Row, 1975), page 79.

2. Maggie Scarf, *Unfinished Business: Pressure Points in the Lives of Women* (New York: Ballantine Books, 1980), page 522.

3. Peggy Harrar, "The Gift of Dependency—A Daughter's Reflections," in *Change*, newsletter of the National Support Center for Families of the Aging (Swarthmore, PA: Summer 1984, No. 3), page 1.

The Skills of Active Loving

"Take my yoke upon you, and learn from me; for I am gentle and lowly in heart, and you will find rest for your souls. For my yoke is easy, and my burden is light."
Matthew 11:29-30, RSV; emphasis added

47

What can you learn from Jesus that will help your caregiving? He says if you learn it, your burden will be light.

If you're feeling burdened, you may already have tried and failed to be more like Jesus—you haven't been able to make yourself more loving, more faithful, more self-denying—and the harder you work at it, the worse you feel about yourself.

I don't say this to burden you even more, but to reassure you that there are things you can learn that will help you relate to your parent in new and better ways. They have nothing to do with trying to manufacture more loving feelings, and everything to do with practical communications skills that anyone can master.

What do these practical skills have to do with God?

Simply put, God acts. But human beings react.

We humans are always waiting to see what others do and say, and then we react accordingly. If others like us, we warm up to them. If we think they don't, we withdraw. If someone says something that touches a sensitive spot (one of our "hot buttons"), we get angry. If we feel unappreciated, our feelings get hurt.

God simply is. He acts according to His nature, not according to whether He's being well received. He loves no matter how we may react to His love. He sends rain on "the just and the unjust alike."

In the gospel accounts, Jesus shows us how to be like this. He acts. He doesn't wait to see how the woman at the well will receive His message before talking to her. And when He listens, He hears people—He's not distracted by His own emotional reactions to them, nor by their surface appearances. He gets beneath the surface and responds to what they're really feeling.

While you can never be perfect imitators of Christ, you can improve the way you relate to the people you're caring for by learning to act more and react less. This means that you focus more on the opportunities in your relationship and less on the problems. Victims don't act; they're acted upon. Are you feeling trapped and victimized? Whenever you can take the initiative in a situation, you can stop feeling like a victim.

I call these *active* loving (as opposed to reactive loving) skills. These skills, which anyone can learn, are

▶ Active listening,
▶ Nonverbal touching, and
▶ Giving positive reinforcement.

An additional component of active loving, setting limits, is discussed in the next chapter. Together, they become the means of *ministering* to your parent in her old age.

ACTIVE LISTENING

"He heard the cry of the afflicted" (Job 34:28, RSV). The Hebrew word translated "heard" really is closer to the English word *listened.* It means "attend to" and (by implication) "respond to." Since God knows our hearts, when He listens He attends not only to the words we say, but to what we are feeling deep inside. We are not God and we cannot know with certainty what people are feeling, but we can learn to hear "the cry of the afflicted," even when it's disguised behind angry words and ugly behavior. As we learn to listen with our hearts as well as with our ears, we become more godly people. "Active listening" is another name for this.

Active listening will help you to break the habit of responding predictably when your parent pushes one of your hot buttons. It can help you to break out of the circular communications trap that so many families are in—going round and round about the same old things.

Let me warn you: This sounds so deceptively simple that you may not believe it will work. Try it! You'll also find that it's much more difficult than it looks because it's not the way human beings normally communicate with each other. Keep practicing! In time, it will change the way you and your parent relate to each other because it is based on the same kind of deep listening that God uses.

Perhaps the best way to introduce the technique of active listening is to give some sample dialogues. I have listed some of the things that a parent will typically say, followed by the response a caregiver would normally make, and then that of an active listener:

Parent: I don't know what to do with myself all day long.

Normal response: I've suggested lots of things, but you don't want to try any of them.

Active listening response: It sounds to me like you're feeling down because you're not doing anything that interests you.

Parent: I'm all alone. Nobody cares about me.

Normal response: I care.

Active listening response: It sounds to me like you're feeling isolated from people.

Parent: The doctor wants me to go in the hospital. I'll probably never leave.

Normal response: Don't worry; you're going to be fine.

Active listening response: Are you afraid?

Parent: I'm no good for anything anymore. Why don't you just throw me in a hole?

Normal response: Don't talk like that!

Active listening response: It sounds to me like you're afraid we might want to get rid of you.

What is the major difference between the active listening response and the normal response? The active listener reflects back the speaker's own feelings, as if in a mirror. That's why it's sometimes called reflective listening.

The first time or two that you try this, you may feel like an idiot. Your parent says, "I'm so nervous. I keep hearing these noises at night," and you say, "You feel nervous because you hear noises at night." You've become Little Sir Echo. What good does this do?

For one thing, your parent may feel, for the first time in her life, that someone is really listening to her. This is a novel experience for most people. Normally, people don't really listen to each other. They listen with half an ear, waiting for an opportunity to talk. They miss the most important part of the message—the emotional content. In the last example above, the message was not about noises. It was about the mother's fear, loneliness, and anxiety.

"What's the good of talking about that?" you may ask.

Some of the complaints that adult children have about their parents—the elders' sadness, listlessness, stubbornness, complaining, and critical and demanding behavior—are a reaction not to aging but to grief. You may not realize that your parent is grieving the loss of her driver's license, independence, or eyesight. If you listen attentively, your parent may be able to work through this grief, and the problem behavior may simply fade away.

Your parent is no different from any other human being. When she is able to talk about her emotions, she not only feels better but she begins to get a handle on them. The only problem is that nobody really wants to know about her feelings. To be alone with feelings that you can't handle and nobody will acknowledge is one of the worst trials of old age.

Acknowledge Feelings

One of the responses above, "Don't worry," is a way of saying, "I don't really want to know about what you feel." This type of easy reassurance cuts your parent short. What might happen if you responded at the feeling level by saying, "Are you afraid?"

Your parent might deny that he's afraid.

Your parent might correct you: "No, I'm not afraid; I feel
_____."

Your parent might talk about specific fears that you could
give reassurance about. For example, if he's afraid there won't
be enough money to pay for an operation, you could investi-
gate and reassure him about that.

Your parent may be thinking about his own possible
death and want to talk about a will or funeral arrangements.

Talking about a parent's death makes most adult children
very uncomfortable. But it's very necessary. Your parent is not
being morbid. He's facing his own mortality realistically,
which is something everyone must do. If you can bring yourself
to face it with him, you'll make him feel less alone, and you'll
also take a giant step yourself toward greater maturity.

Active Listening Is Not a Panacea

I'm not promising that active listening will "cure" your parent
of complaining. The following dialogue is probably typical of
what takes place in many nursing homes:

> Parent: I hate this place; I'm nothing but a prisoner.
> Caregiver: It sounds to me like you're angry about
> being here.
> Parent: You're darned right I'm angry. Why don't
> you do something about it? Why don't you get me out
> of here?

For some caregivers this dialogue can take place every
day. When the subject comes up, you could be tempted to
retell all the reasons why you can't remove her from the
nursing home that she's heard over and over. But what are
some alternative responses? You could say, "I'm sorry," giving
her a hug, "but this is the best I can do."

"I can understand why you're so angry. I'm sure I'd feel
the same way if I were in your shoes." (Say this also with a
hug.)

"Mother, this anger is normal. It sounds like you're

grieving for your lost independence."

The last response may help her identify the reason for some of her emotion. She probably doesn't realize that she's grieving and that anger is a normal part of the grieving process. This doesn't, however, mean that she'll stop being angry. Unfortunately, some people are "stuck" in the angry stage for a long, long time!

However, even if she does remain angry, you've stepped out of your old pattern of repeatedly arguing and reasoning with her. That doesn't help her and it's extremely frustrating for you.

Some Important Don'ts

Don't correct. Sometimes elderly parents exaggerate, misstate, or misremember; it drives their adult children crazy. They feel compelled to set the record straight. What they don't understand is that the distortion is there because the parent is reporting not facts but feelings.

The parent who accuses a grandchild of stealing her social security check really feels that something has been stolen from her, like her health or her freedom. A check, which she may have misplaced, becomes a convenient substitute object for her feelings. When an elder who has been alone for an hour says, "I've been alone all day," he really means that times hangs so heavy on his hands that it feels like all day.

As long as you're correcting, you're not really listening to the feelings.

Don't attempt to argue your parent out of his feelings. There is nothing worse than being told that your feelings are not valid. That means that you, as a person, are not okay. Your parent knows how he feels. Saying, "You don't really mean that" or "How could you feel that way," will only encourage him to keep his feelings bottled up inside where they can do the most harm.

Don't judge. We've all been taught (perhaps by the very parent we're taking care of) that certain feelings are acceptable and others are not. Unfortunately, Christians are often the quickest to condemn the "unacceptable" feelings. But the feeling is not the sin. (Ephesians 4:26 [RSV] says, "Be angry but do not sin," so obviously, the anger is not the sin.) It's what you do with the unacceptable feeling that's potentially sinful. Your judgment—which besides being unhelpful is unscriptural—will only drive the elder's feelings deeper underground.

Don't feel you have to solve the problem. That's demeaning to your parents. If they're mentally competent, they don't need you to solve their problems; they need to be heard. Responsible adults will almost always solve their own problems if given time to talk them through. If your parent expects you to solve her problems, you may have made her too dependent on you. Back off and ask questions that will draw her out, such as, "What are your options?"

Don't give advice. A twin of the impulse to solve the problem is the impulse, almost the compulsion, to give advice. It feels so good to the advice-giver! But it only makes the advice-taker more dependent and helpless, giving her someone to blame if it doesn't work. People don't really want advice, even when they ask for it. Often, asking for advice is the only way they know to start a conversation about their problem. Instead of giving advice, ask open-ended questions to draw her out.

Don't try to cheer her up. This is similar to giving well-meant, but hasty, reassurance. It cuts off the full expression of her feelings. She may, perhaps, cheer up after she's talked out her feelings. Frequently, when you get feelings out in the open, you do feel better. But she has to go through this—don't choke off the process.

Don't say, "I know just how you feel." This is presumptuous. You are not in her shoes and can't really know how she feels. Besides, this is another way of cutting her short. If you already know how she feels, it's not necessary for her to tell you.

When you begin actively listening to your parent and reflecting back her feelings, you may find yourself communicating with your parent at a deep level about things that really matter. You'll feel very close—perhaps for the first time in a long time or for the first time ever. The "normal" response protects you from a closeness that many people find uncomfortable. As long as you keep communications at their normal, superficial level, you won't have to change.

It May Be Painful

Change and growth sometimes cause pain (pain is perhaps an inevitable part of growth), and refusing to listen to a parent is a way of avoiding it. If the parent is honest about his feelings, we may not always like what we hear. A lot of negative emotions may get vented. But sometimes it's necessary to let out some of the negative emotions before more positive ones can appear.

Should you listen to the same negative statements over and over? If necessary you should, but you'll probably find they fade out in time. Usually, active listening draws out the speaker to explore his feelings. It elicits less of the "broken record" type of communication than does a normal response.

Should you allow yourself to be attacked? Sometimes active listening is the best way to respond to what seems like an attack. It deflects attention away from you and back to what the attacker is feeling.

Parent: You're late again!
Caregiver, active listener: It sounds like you're really anxious to see me.

However, I don't think you should listen to what amounts to abuse of you as a person. Remind your parent that you're an adult and deserve to be spoken to with respect. And, of course, always speak to her with respect. If you do not talk to her as if she were a child—scolding, blaming, etc.—she's more likely to respond on an adult level.

Nor should you respond to attacks on third persons. Instead, say, "That's between you and him; I don't want to hear about it," or "Why don't you tell him that yourself?"

Short-Circuiting the Hot Buttons

Active listening enables you to step back from your habitual reactions to your parent. In most parent-child relationships, one is pushing the other's buttons in order to gain control. The following are some examples:

Button parent is pushing	Your reaction
Disapproving look; disapproval button	Give in; "I must have approval."
Critical statement; criticism button	Anger; bingo—she scored a hit.
Verbal put down; self-esteem button	Feel worthless; she controls my feelings of self-worth.
Guilt statement; guilt button	Guilt; must atone by doing what she wants.

Let's take a guilt-inducing type of statement:

Parent: I've been alone all day.
        Caregiver: It sounds like you've been feeling lonely.

Notice what happened. The parent feels lonely; you didn't make her feel lonely by leaving her alone. She could have chosen a different reaction. Who's responsible, you or she? She is. She owns her feelings of loneliness, not you. She pushed the guilt button, but you short-circuited it. If you had responded by becoming defensive—"I was only gone for an hour!"—you'd be agreeing to assume responsibility for her feelings. As soon as you do that, you've made a tacit agreement to feel guilty if she's unhappy about something.

A very important part of accepting your parent is letting go of things you can do nothing about. This is impossible as long as you, the caregiver, hold yourself responsible for your parent's feelings.

Ask yourself, "Am I responsible for the fact that she's

eighty-six and frail?" "Did I give her Parkinson's disease?" "Is it my fault that institutional care isn't like being home?"

Try practicing a few key sentences in front of a mirror until you feel confident you can say them to your parent: "I'm sorry that you don't like it, but I can't help it." "There's nothing I can do about it."

Your parent must also learn to accept what cannot be changed. If she can't, you can't do it for her. In the last analysis, everybody has to take responsibility for her own feelings about whatever happens to her.

GIVE LOVE BEFORE IT'S DEMANDED

One of the hardest things in the world to do is to give love to a parent who's critical and demanding. So the adult child pulls back. The less she gives, the more the parent demands, and so on. Someone must break this vicious cycle, and it might as well be you.

Humanly speaking, it's normal for you to resent giving love on demand. From your parent's point of view, love extracted from someone under duress is always suspect. ("She doesn't really love me, or I wouldn't have had to ask her for it.") When you give love before it's demanded, you gain more control. Furthermore, love freely given is so much more satisfying to the recipient that she may be able to ease up on her demands.

However, giving love and setting limits must go hand in hand. In saying, "Give love before it's demanded," I'm not saying, "Give in to every demand in order to keep peace." For example:

Your parent who lives independently calls you several times a day. The phone calls disrupt your work and your family life. You acknowledge her loneliness, but the frequent calls continue.

Do you say, "Don't call," and hurt her feelings?

Do you say nothing and allow frustration and resentment to build up?

A better approach is to chart the calls. What time of day are they most frequent? This may be a time when she's feeling most anxious. Then you can call her before she has a chance to call you—at the time when she feels most anxious and down. Is there some concern or complaint that keeps recurring? Pick a time to call when you can listen to her discuss some concern at length. Or you arrange to go see her, planning to take the time to actively listen to her about this concern.

At the same time, you lovingly explain that you can't talk to her on the phone so often, but that you'll be calling her once a day, or twice a week (or as often as you feel comfortable), when you will be free to talk at least twenty minutes or longer. You're sure that you'll both enjoy long talks when you're not distracted much more than a lot of short calls. It may take time, but if you're firm and stick to your decision, the situation will change. In order to reinforce your decision, you may have to put an answering machine on your home phone, if you do not already have one.

You may not realize how much you can do to help yourself in these situations. But in order to *stop feeling like a victim,* you must *take the initiative.*

USE NONVERBAL TOUCHING

One of the best ways to improve a situation involving a critical and demanding parent is to use nonverbal communications, the most powerful of which is touch.

In the opening chapter of his moving book *Making Peace with Your Parents,* Dr. Harold H. Bloomfield tells how he began healing his relationship with his father through hugging him.

His first attempts met resistance. He and his father had never shown affection to each other; his father tensed up. Dr. Bloomfield persisted, saying, "Come on, Dad, I really want to hug you." Letting go of his own resentment, he kept trying, encouraging his father to hug him back, even giving him instructions for doing so. By the two hundredth hug, his father was enjoying the hugs and even said "I love you" for the first time that he could remember.[1]

I don't know if many of us could do what Dr. Bloomfield did. If your parent tenses up when you try to hug him, your hurt from this rejection could make it very difficult for you to persist. But there are other ways of touching. Your parent needs it, and so do you. The skin is the body's largest sense organ with millions of nerve endings. Without stimulation of the skin, human beings often experience an ache or longing that the medical world labels "skin hunger." Whether or not you are touched can make a measurable physical difference to your body. Unfortunately, often nobody touches the elderly at a time when they've suffered many losses and need touching the most.

Many Ways of Touching

Listen to Alice, a New York caregiver:

"My mother is so undemonstrative. I tried to comfort her, but it was like holding a piece of wood." If your parent responds coldly or not at all to your attempts at hugging, don't give up. You can still

▶ pat her shoulder, squeeze her arm, take her hand in yours,
▶ give a backrub,
▶ rub lotion on dry areas of her skin,
▶ give a massage,
▶ brush her hair, and
▶ offer your arm when you walk together.

If, for some reason, you can't do any of these (you may have hurts that are still unhealed), don't feel you must. You can encourage other family members to hug your parent. Perhaps you can encourage her to get a pet. Do what you can. As you are able to bring yourself to do more touching, you'll feel better, too.

GIVE POSITIVE REINFORCEMENT

Instead of focusing on your parents' problems, it's frequently more useful to think about ways to help them raise their self-esteem. It's impossible to argue older people out of their feelings of worthlessness. But when people are able to feel better about themselves, feelings of worthlessness and problem behaviors can simply melt away. There are many ways to give your parents positive reinforcement that will help to raise their self-esteem. Your active listening is one of them. Other methods include the following:

Allow Her to Give as Well as Receive

In the past, your mother may have derived a large part of her self-esteem from doing things for her family; now her family tells her, "You sit down, Mom, we'll do it." But if she's still physically and mentally capable, you're doing her no kindness by making her feel useless.

Instead of focusing on what she can't do, encourage her to do what she can. If she can no longer cook for family gatherings, can she still set the table? Heat food in a microwave oven? Fold napkins or other laundry? Polish silver? So what if she's very slow, and you could do it much faster yourself. Which is more important—getting everything done quickly and efficiently, or helping her self-esteem?

If she misses something while dusting or makes a mistake in setting a table, don't do the task over in her presence so that she feels no longer "good enough."

Help Her Adapt to Handicaps

In chapter 8, you'll find tips for adapting to handicaps that come with aging, such as failing eyesight or hearing or decreased physical mobility. These adaptations make it possible for the elderly to continue doing activities they enjoy.

For example, failing eyesight doesn't mean your mother has to give up cooking. If she has enough sensitivity in her fingertips, Braille dials can be put on the stove. If her arthritic hands make crocheting impossible, perhaps she can try latch-hooking, since the latch hook doesn't require finger movement and coordination; it can be held in the fist.

Perhaps your father loved to putter in the yard but no longer has the strength or can no longer walk. With plants in raised beds and boxes, he can garden sitting down or from a wheelchair. If he loves carpentry but can't see well, there are computerized "talking tools" and rulers with Braille markers.

If your parents can no longer see well enough to write letters, they can "write" to family members by talking into a tape recorder. Or, if you keep them supplied with cards and stamps, they can send cards on important occasions even from a nursing home and always remember important dates in others' lives.

Show Your Parent She Is Valued
The best way to encourage your parent to continue doing what she can is to value what she does. Proudly displaying a gift that an elder has made or telling others (in your parent's presence) that you're proud of your parent builds self-esteem. Give her credit (in her hearing) for something she's taught you that you or your children do well. Can she still teach a skill? Find some way in which she can do this. Be generous with your praise.

Craft fairs at which elders can sell what they've made are important, not just to help older people earn a little extra money, but to help raise their self-esteem. When Sally's mother entered a retirement home, one of the first things Sally did was to bring over and set up her mother's sewing machine. Even though she could no longer make clothing for her family, Sally's mom continued to make small items that could be sold in the home's gift shop. I used to visit a retirement home in which one lady still knitted busily. Every visitor got a bright red or blue pot holder to take home.

Allow Them to Give Memories
Old people have so much to give—especially their memories. Fortunately for Lucy, her daughter Katie is a history buff and

president of her local historical society. Lucy is a member of a pioneer family that helped settle their hometown.

After her mother came to live with her, Katie began recording Lucy's memories of her childhood. She contacted the rangers at the town's living history site and they also interviewed Lucy. She was a prominent guest at a Fourth of July celebration at the historical site and at the town's "Pioneer Days" celebration. By her ninetieth birthday, Lucy had become a local celebrity.

Capture Your Parent on Tape

Obviously, taping isn't possible for everybody. But if it is possible for you to capture your parent's early memories on audio- or videotape, what a treasure this will be for your children in years to come. One of my deepest regrets is that nobody ever wrote down my father's recollections of World War I. He was an infantryman who participated in almost every major battle, but by the time he was elderly he'd lost interest in retelling his war stories. They're gone forever.

My mother was equally reluctant to talk about her past. Her attitude was that it was over and done with; she didn't want to think about it anymore. Yet my daughter was able to persuade her to record some of her recollections on cassette tape. They were, much to my amazement, very positive memories.

"How come I heard only the bad stuff about her past and you got all the good stuff?" I asked my daughter.

"Because you're the daughter and I'm the granddaughter," she laughed.

Now, that seems a little unfair. Nevertheless, I'm grateful to have that tape and grateful to my daughter for doing this for all of us. Perhaps if your parent resists taping memories for you, another family member can persuade her.

Life Stories

You may find, in stationery and gift shops, fill-in-the-blank books called "Grandma's Memories" or "Grandpa's Memories."

These provide room for certain standard facts such as where he was born, where he went to school, etc. They're fine as far as they go, but it's possible to do a great deal more.

Some elders (or their caregivers) with a flair for writing have taken their tape recorded memories and produced books that make priceless family gifts. With today's printing technology, publishing a book is not as expensive nor as arduous as you may think.

If you have access to a computer and desktop publishing software, you can produce typeset pages, complete with graphics, that you can take to a print shop. If not, the typewritten or word-processed copy will have to be pasted up on boards to be made ready for the printer. If you want headlines and titles, they'll have to be typeset. Any black-and-white photos will have to be screened (your print shop will take care of this for you) and then pasted up. There will be additional charges for typesetting and screening.

You will need to take your camera-ready copy to several printers for bids, since charges will vary a great deal. Some printers can bind your books for you. If they can't, you'll have to take the printed pages to a bindery.

If you don't feel you have the skills for this, you might be able to find someone who provides this service as a small business. I've seen several of these and they are delightful. Anybody would be proud and happy to have one as a keepsake of a relative.

THE IMPORTANCE OF THE LIFE REVIEW

When you encourage your parent to write down or record his or her memories, you are helping with something that gerontologists say is very important to the elderly: the life review. The life review helps the elderly to discover the meaning of their lives. Dr. Robert N. Butler, a gerontologist who coined the phrase "life review," points out that the tendency of the elderly to live in the past is not unhealthy unless the past begins to totally blot out the present. Orderly reminiscing is a necessary part of coming to terms with one's life and should not be discouraged.

If you have been troubled by your parent's tendency to turn to the past, it's helpful to know that it's okay for him to do so. You may see this tendency as something very negative, and at times it can be. His reminiscence may lead to dwelling on past mistakes, hurts, and wrongs, i.e., "I should haves" and "If onlys." Here's where you can help by asking questions.

"What do you think that meant in your life?" "How did you feel when that happened?" and "Did anything good come out of that?" are the types of questions that may lead him to see his life in a new way.

See if you can express admiration for his courage. For example, you could say, "Gee, I never knew the Depression was so rough. I can't believe what a great job you did raising us with so little to work with."

As you get to know your parent better through his reminiscing, you may discover many positive qualities that you either were not aware of or never before showed your appreciation for. For example, my mother was very stubborn. (No doubt that's what kept her going until age eighty-nine despite a lifetime of poor health.) Once, I remember saying to her admiringly, "You never give up, do you? Most people would have given up long ago. But you're so determined. You just keep plugging away."

She didn't say anything, but I could see that she was pleased. And I wasn't trying to flatter her. I honestly did have a newly found appreciation of a quality in her that sometimes made her very hard to deal with. Your reaction to your parent's stories—in fact, anybody's reaction—provides feedback that's helpful to a productive life review.

It may help to prepare yourself, in advance of visiting your parent, with topics to reminisce about. For example, you could start a conversation about child rearing in the old days or home remedies for illnesses or what his first job was like. The possibilities are endless. Encourage the memory of as much detail as possible; this will make the stories more vivid.

If detailed recollections are slow to come, you can frequently prime the pump by going over old pictures with your parent. Or if you have him replay a tape he's made, this may stimulate additional memories. A psychologist who works with the elderly and their families, Dr. Richard P. Johnson, has invented a board game called "Generations" designed to help adult children work with their parents on life reviews. (See the Appendix for where to order it.) You might want to try this if you have difficulty getting started.

Spiritual Dimensions of the Life Review
Occasionally, material that is painful will come up in reminiscences. Your parent will have a need to forgive someone or perhaps be forgiven, and this can be very difficult. Perhaps this need has him "stuck," unable to move on. I hesitate to advise anyone to become his parent's spiritual counselor, although some individuals can play this role. In most cases, this problem is much better handled by a trusted clergyman, a spiritually mature friend, or someone not as emotionally tied to your parent as you are.

FINDING THE TIME

If you have read these suggestions, you may be shaking your head and thinking, "How will I ever find the time to do all that?"

You don't have to follow up every suggestion. Also, many of these suggestions take little additional time. You can reminisce with your parent or give a backrub or a massage during the course of a regular visit. And lastly, when you do the fun things for and with your parent and hire someone else to do the routine tasks, more positive feelings will begin to flow between you. You'll have more energy. (You'll be amazed how much energy you were using just to keep a lid on your negative emotions.)

When you become a caregiver, you have to think long term, not short term. In the short term, it may be possible to do everything yourself, to keep meeting your parent's needs and even her demands as they arise. But in the long run, this is not possible. Caregiving can last for years. The best way for you to find the time and energy to give your parent emotional support is to get help and learn to take care of yourself so you don't burn out.

NOTE: 1. Harold H. Bloomfield, M.D., with Leonard Felder, Ph.D., *Making Peace with Your Parents: The Key to Enriching Your Life and All Your Relationships* (New York: Ballantine Books, 1983), pages 5-6.

4

Is Self-Preservation Wrong?

*Choose life, that you and your
descendants may live.*
Deuteronomy 30:19, RSV

*"For I know the plans I have for
you," declares the LORD, "plans to
prosper you and not to harm you,
plans to give you hope and a
future."*
Jeremiah 29:11

"You, too, have a right to live!"

These words, spoken by my pastor during a counseling session shortly after I became a caregiver, helped to bring me to my senses.

Tears sprang to my eyes. Until that moment, I wasn't sure that another human being in the world thought that I, too, deserved to live—not my fellow church members, not my friends, not my mother, not my children, not even my husband. Maybe not even God.

Judging by the way many caregivers feel and act, they, too, doubt their own right to live. I see them single-mindedly carrying out their caregiving duties while neglecting their own bodies, minds, and spirits. In time, they become caught in a downward spiral of negative thinking and unhealthy living that is deadly in every sense of the word.

Many caregivers are extraordinarily sensitive to sermons on the beauty of self-sacrifice and the dangers of selfishness, and either are not exposed to or do not hear any teachings on their own worth. If each person is precious in God's sight, then it is not part of His plan to take care of one generation by requiring the sacrifice of another. Everybody's needs must be balanced, including the needs of the caregiver. It is never wrong to want to live and to reach out for help in order to do so. In fact, the ability to ask for help is a sign of health, not sickness. Caregiving is not synonymous with martyrdom.

If the way you're giving care is pleasing to God, you'll be a physically healthy and emotionally and spiritually strong human being. If your manner of caregiving is an unhealthy one, motivated mainly by your desire to live up to society's expectations or your own prideful self-image, you'll become sick and depressed, suffer in your relationships with others, become cut off from fellowship with God, and find it difficult to pray or read Scripture. You'll be isolated and joyless—and if you really hit rock bottom, longing for death. It's much easier to prevent this than to pull yourself out of this hole once you're in it.

SCRIPTURAL SELF-CARE

Scripture does not urge believers to care for themselves; it simply assumes that they will do so. In Ephesians, the Apostle Paul urges husbands to love their wives as they love their own bodies: "For no man ever hates his own flesh, but nourishes and cherishes it" (Ephesians 5:29, RSV). And Jesus said, "love your neighbor as yourself" (Matthew 19:19). Scriptural self-care is based on God's action in creating and loving us. Because He made us, we are worth preserving. In chapter 2, I asked you to see your parent as God sees him or her—that is, objectively, as he or she really is. Can you also see yourself as God sees you? If so, then you will see someone who is worthy of being loved and cared for.

The most important thing you have to give your parent is yourself. You can easily become so drained from the physical care of a parent that you have nothing left to give her emotionally or spiritually.

Bessie took dinner to her mother every day. While she was there, Bessie cleaned the apartment, gathered up dirty laundry, looked at bills, and did many little things. Yet no matter how long she was there, her mother always thought up extra jobs to keep her longer.

Bessie was exasperated—until a wise social worker pointed out that her mother wanted companionship and emotional support. Bessie's mother would be much happier if Bessie sat down with her mother while she ate, talked to her, listened to her, and either let some of the housework go or found someone else to do it.

When you are too exhausted from many tasks to give of yourself emotionally, your loved one will suffer. You must find a way to keep your own well filled if you are to continue to give without running dry. That means not only taking care of yourself so that you don't get drained faster than God can fill you up, but also drawing closer to God so that you are relying on the Living Water and not your own resources.

Heed the advice of Joan, a Connecticut caregiver: "If I

could say just one thing to other caregivers, it would be, 'Find time to be by yourself and listen to God.' I need that quiet time, and I used to take it first thing in the morning. Then when John's mother came to live with us, our entire schedule changed. Now when I get up, she's already up, waiting for breakfast. So I had to find a new time to be alone, and that took a while. But things are much better now that I'm doing this again."

You also need to give yourself positive messages from the Scriptures. Fill your mind with verses such as Psalm 121:2: "My help comes from the LORD." Pain and tragedy are inevitable in this fallen world, but God's help is ever near, unless you become too depressed to reach out for it.

If you are searching the Scriptures and finding only condemnation instead of hope, remember that the Devil can also quote Scripture. The habit of condemning yourself for your feelings gives him ammunition to use against you.

Judy didn't want to go and visit her mother, who had broken her hip. Judy was exhausted from working, she needed time for herself, and she resented the fact that she now had to drive a hundred miles to visit her mother in the hospital. She went anyway, but for months she condemned herself for her unwillingness to go.

Remember the parable of the man who had two sons (Matthew 21:28-32)? He asked both to work in the vineyard. One said yes, but didn't go. The other at first said no, but later changed his mind and went. Jesus praised the obedient son. Which one was that? The one who went, of course. Whether or not he felt like going was beside the point. Jesus never condemned him for his feelings. Now apply the same reasoning to yourself.

Condemning yourself for perfectly natural and normal feelings only prevents you from admitting them to God and letting go of them. This is a bondage that keeps you separated from God.

In addition to God, you also need other people. If you become isolated with your elderly parent, you will suffer from loneliness, low self-image, and boredom. Your depressed state will inevitably affect your loved one, who will then feel like a burden and become increasingly depressed and difficult, which will make you feel more depressed. If this is already happening, you need to reverse this vicious cycle as soon as possible. You can do this by making some conscious decisions.

Decision 1: Decide to Live

We need to be in touch with our own needs and our feelings; people who deny their needs and feelings lose touch with themselves and with God. It is *not* selfish to recognize that we have needs. God put those needs within us. To deny that they are there is to deny the life He gave us and to choose death for ourselves instead of life. If you have taken a caregiving role, you've certainly put another's needs ahead of your own, but that's no reason to deny your needs. Because you prepare food for your family, does this mean that you shouldn't eat, too? Of course not.

When you admit that you can't handle it alone, that you're hurting and need help, you've made a decision to live.

"How do you feel?" I asked a caregiver on the phone.

"Lousy!" she said.

"Praise the Lord," I said under my breath. This was the first time she'd ever admitted that she wasn't just fine. A seriously depressed person who hid her pain behind a pasted-on smile, she'd just taken the first step toward reaching out for help.

Decision 2: Ask for Help

Caregivers are often reluctant to ask even close family members for help. I don't think this is abnormal; to ask for help is to risk rejection. And to ask for help is also to admit that you're not invulnerable and perfect—and that will hurt your pride.

You don't understand why others don't *offer* to help before you have to ask. But did you understand what caregivers went through before you took on the role? I doubt it. It's your responsibility to communicate—if possible, in a calm, loving manner—what you and the elder need. Even then, your listeners may not know what *they* can do to help. Be ready with a list of specific suggestions. Make a list of the tasks you do for your loved one. Present this list and ask which tasks your relatives could take over and which you could pay someone to do. If you need financial assistance in hiring help, don't hesitate to ask for that, too.

"I'm so worn out," said Abby, a young friend of mine in Tennessee whose grandmother was living with her. "Big Mama has six children, including two sons in the same town, but I do everything."

"Did you ever ask your uncles for help?"

Just as I'd suspected, she hadn't. When she did, one of her uncles said, "Why, baby, you never said anything, so I thought y'all were getting along just fine." He began taking his mother out for lunch once a week and gave Abby money to hire help—which he could well afford and she could not.

You may be preventing your relatives from doing anything by doing too much. Try creating some space in your caregiving. Sometimes it will be filled, even by unwilling family members.

Cathy's mother was in a board-and-care home. Cathy, even though she worked full time, was the sole caregiver. Her brother, who lived nearby, almost never put in an appearance. One holiday weekend, Cathy (who was fed up with her brother) decided to go away for a couple of days without telling him or her mother's board-and-care home where she was going. (The home had her brother's home number as well as hers for use in emergencies.)

"What can happen in three days?" she thought.

While Cathy was gone, her mom fell. The home's staff called her brother. For the first time, he saw his mother in pain and fear and felt her anger directed against him. He called her former doctor, who refused to come and then contacted another doctor and talked him into meeting him at the emergency room. Because Cathy's brother was forced to cope, he did.

"You know," Cathy chuckled, "he's now much more sympathetic to me than he used to be."

What Cathy had done, by withdrawing her presence on this particular weekend, was to create a vacuum in her mother's care into which her brother—whether he liked it or not—was drawn. This might happen more often if caregivers didn't insist on doing it all themselves.

If a parent has been used to having you do everything, he may protest that he doesn't want any other help. This may be very flattering, but get help anyway. It's normal for sick and/or frail people to become self-centered; they may have no idea what unrelieved caregiving may be doing to you. In the long run, you have to look out for both his and your best interests, and it is not in his best interests for you to burn out and collapse.

Decision 3: Give Up the Need to Be in Control

Some caregivers have an ungodly need to control the circumstances of their loved ones' lives. I've heard caregivers say things such as, "If I do everything I can, God will give me the strength to take care of Mom at home, and she'll never have to go into a nursing home."

Funny, but I don't remember reading any open-ended promises like that in *my* Bible. Where does it say that if we put out enough effort, God owes us something? Beware: The line between faith and presumption is a very thin one, and many caregivers may unwittingly have crossed it.

If you have the mistaken belief that you, and not God, are in control of your parent's circumstances, this is based on some commonly held false beliefs. For example, you may say, "I am responsible for Mom's happiness." The truth, however, is that each person is responsible for his own happiness. A corollary is "I am responsible for Mom's health." The truth is that each mentally competent person is responsible for his own health. False belief: "If I don't do it, nobody else will." The truth: often, what you really mean is, "If I don't do it, I will no longer be in control." False belief: "If I do it right, I'll get the love and respect and appreciation I deserve." The truth is that you may receive anger and hostility rather than appreciation.

What happens when you stop trying to do and control everything is that you give God some room to work. I've seen many miracles happen when caregivers are finally able to move themselves out of God's way.

Decision 4: Learn to Set Limits

What is your long-term goal? Is it to keep your parent functioning well as long as possible? If you allow yourself to burn out, won't that hasten the day when she may have to be institutionalized? Setting limits will help you to prevent this.

To set limits is to assess realistically (1) what your parent needs (not wants); (2) how many of these needs you can meet, taking into account your responsibilities to yourself and other family members; and (3) who besides yourself can meet some of these needs.

When you set limits, you have to say no to some of your parent's wants. You can't give her everything she wants. You may not even be able to give her everything she needs. This hurts, but that's just the way it is.

When setting limits, think of your caregiving not as personal service but as "care managing." The professional care manager is a worker who figures out how to meet the client's (in this case, your parent's) needs and then hires or calls in others in the community to provide services. (I'll have more to say about where to find these services in chapter 8.)

Setting limits is the loving thing to do. When Jane's strength ran out, she put her mother in a nearby board-and-care home.

"I'm free to love my mother again," Jane said.

She meant that now that she was no longer exhausted from giving around-the-clock care, she could enjoy her mother's company. Your parent might be better off with a cheerful, rested caregiver who enjoys being with her than an exhausted and resentful one who can't give her the emotional support she needs. Your ability to set limits will determine which it will be.

Limits are a form of security. Your parent may be relieved when you let her know where they are. Some parents may be just testing to find the limits. *Not* finding any will make them anxious and fearful. If you find yourself unable to set any, this may indicate a problem within you that needs to be dealt with.

An example of limit-setting is how you handle disruptive phone calls. If your parent calls several times a day, disrupting your family's life, and nothing you say and no reassurance you give seems to help, you may have to get a telephone answering machine. Then you can talk to her when you choose to and when it's convenient for you.

Decision 5: Schedule Time for Yourself

The best way to find time for yourself is to use techniques of time management. Make a list of things you have to do daily, weekly, monthly, or whenever, and prioritize them. If there are more things on your list than there are hours in the day, you must not eliminate the things essential to your own health and well-being. Anything you don't have time to do personally will either have to be done by someone else—another family member, volunteer, or hired person—or be left undone.

Prepare charts for each day of the week for at least one month at a time and block out time needed for sleeping, eating (including shopping for and preparing meals), and exercise. Next write in your top priority items: (1) time alone with God; (2) time to do at least one thing you enjoy; (3) time to relax; and if you're married, (4) time for your spouse and/or children.

None of these has to be large blocks of time. Ten minutes of concentrated Bible reading and prayer is preferable to an hour of anxious "study" with a wandering mind.

Make appointments with yourself—and keep them. Doing something every day that gives you pleasure will help to restore your spirit. It doesn't have to be anything big. If growing plants gives you pleasure, buy and nurture a new flowering plant and watch it grow. If creating something with needlework renews you, start a project that you can carry with you and work on in the time you spend in doctors' waiting rooms. Something that you do for yourself can be as simple as talking on the phone to a friend, getting your hair styled at the beauty parlor, or writing in your journal.

The key is to schedule enjoyment and to keep that appointment before you dribble away the entire day in all the urgent tasks that need to be done—but which drain you instead of renewing you.

Decision 6: Care for Your Physical Body

One of the first places that stress shows up is in your body. If you are gaining or losing weight, have difficulty sleeping, have physical symptoms—headaches, stomachaches, back muscle spasms, high blood pressure, etc.—these are probably signs that you are under stress and need to do something about it. In this life you can't get away from your body—there's no such thing as a serene spirit in a stressed-out body.

Fortunately you can reverse some of the distress in your emotions and spirit by taking care of your body. Exercise relieves tension, helps you eat and sleep better, keeps your heart, lungs, and other bodily organs functioning normally, and lifts your mood. The benefits can be multiplied if you exercise with a friend because then you're taking care of social needs, too. If you're able to exercise vigorously, activities such as digging and chopping in the garden will help you to work off anger.

But exercise doesn't have to be aerobic dancing or cross-country skiing to be effective. Doctors tell us there's no better exercise than walking. Everybody knows how to do it; it requires no fancy clothing or equipment, and it can be done anytime. While you walk, you can be praying, singing a psalm, or praising God for the beauty of the day.

One of our Christian caregivers teamed up with another caregiver she met through our support group, and the two of them started walking early every morning before their mothers, who were late risers, got up. Another caregiver hired a sitter for her mother and joined a local walking club. After their twice-weekly morning walks, members of the club go out for breakfast. The benefits, they reported, are enormous; the hardest part is just getting started. Once you give yourself that push you need, you'll feel so much better that it'll be easier to keep going.

In addition to whatever regular exercise you're getting, you will also benefit from learning and doing specific tension-reducing exercises. Massages, whirlpool baths, and saunas—even hot tubs and showers—help to relax tense muscles. Deep breathing also relieves tension. When you're tense and anxious, you sometimes almost forget to breathe. Shallow breathing doesn't bring enough oxygen to your brain, and you feel tired and dull.

Learn to take "little vacations." This is a form of mental exercise. Lift your eyes from your ever-present tasks and remember a beautiful scene from nature. Take a break and immerse yourself in a favorite piece of music. Look, really look, at your surroundings. Listen to some good advice from one caregiver: "Learn to notice and enjoy the little things"—a beautiful sunrise, the smile on a baby's face at the supermarket, the fresh dew on the grass. Then, with another Christian caregiver, you can say, while in the midst of turmoil: "Life is good!"

Eating the right foods will enable you to function better. It's very common for caregivers, like other people under stress, either to under-eat, to grab "junk" foods on the run, or to stuff themselves and gain a great deal of weight. Food also affects your moods. If you don't want your loved one to have an impatient, irritable caregiver, you need to eat correctly.

Changing your eating habits to include whole grains and fresh fruits and vegetables instead of processed, sugary, salty, and high-fat foods is not easy, but it can be done gradually over time. You may need the support of other people (in a structured program such as Weight Watchers) to make these changes. More and more, you'll see recipes in newspapers and magazines that reflect our increased knowledge of the role played by diet in preventing heart disease, stroke, and cancer. Try them, you'll like them, and you'll also feel better.

Decision 7: Do More Laughing

The Sioux Indians have a proverb: "The first thing a man says after he dies is 'Why was I so serious?'" You can get so bogged down in your caregiving duties that you lose all perspective on life. Laughter will help you restore it.

The Bible says it a little differently: "A merry heart doeth good like a medicine" (Proverbs 17:22, KJV).

This insight has been confirmed in recent times by Norman Cousins, the well-known editor who treated his supposedly incurable disease by watching funny movies. Some hospitals now even have "laughter" rooms for their patients.

If anyone eavesdropped on a Christian Caregivers Support Group meeting, he might be surprised at how much laughing we do. Caregivers need the release of laughter most, and they find it at group meetings when they share their lives with others.

One male caregiver I know whose mother can be very difficult is able to kid her out of her "crotchets" by joking with her. This is an art that all caregivers could profitably cultivate.

If it's hard to find anything funny in your day, look for something to laugh about. Buy a book of cartoons by your favorite cartoonist, look for joke books in the library, or rent a funny video. Then laugh—this will relax both your body and your mind.

Decision 8: Get Away as Often as Possible

At one time, the word *respite* was not even in my vocabulary. But when I became a caregiver, I soon learned that this was what I needed most; it was also the hardest need to satisfy.

The dictionary defines "respite" as (1) a usually short interval of rest or relief; and (2) law, the temporary suspension of a sentence, reprieve. (As a former caregiver, I really appreciate that second definition!)

Getting "respite" is not abandoning your post. It's a short rest or relief that enables you to go on with the performance of your duties, like the "R and R" leaves of the military.

People who have decided to live (decision 1) may have no problem recognizing their need for respite, but they may have trouble figuring out how to get it, whether it's relief for a few hours while they lunch with a friend, relief for a weekend away, or a week's vacation.

The best way to get respite, if other family members are nearby, is to ask for it. Usually, a caregiver's sibling, one of the elder's grandchildren, or a niece or nephew will be happy to stay on a temporary basis. Even if they don't offer, most will do so if asked. The problem is that you may hate to ask, but you have to learn to do so.

If no family is available for respite care, then the options depend on the availability of money, volunteers (friends, church, community), or assistance programs for low-income caregivers who qualify. (This is discussed in detail in chapter 8.) Some nursing homes are now making beds available for short-term respite care. This does not come cheaply, but if your parent agrees, it may be less than the cost of temporary live-in help, which is often unavailable at any price.

In general, getting away regularly is more important than getting away for a long time or going a great distance. What refreshes is a total change in routine; therefore, a weekend camping trip less than a hundred miles from home (provided you like camping) will benefit you as much or more than two weeks in Hawaii. Don't stand on ceremony or hold out for "dream vacations" in some distant future. When an opportunity to get away presents itself, seize it. You don't know what the future holds.

Decision 9: Find the Support You Need

You need emotional support as much as your parent does. You, too, need a place to vent your negative emotions, someone to understand and validate you as a person and someone to be there for you. Some caregivers have ample support from an understanding family, friends, and neighbors. Others are not so fortunate and need to seek out a support group.

For years after becoming a caregiver, it never occurred to me that I might need the help of a support group to cope with my responsibilities. What could a support group do? Caregiving was my problem and I was stuck with it; nothing could change that. Finally, I came to see how stressed-out I was becoming and how desperately I needed to know I was not alone. I prayed for help, and God responded by getting me together with Helen Hight and telling us, "You want a support group? Okay, start your own."

What is a support group?

Typically, it's a group of five to twelve people who share a common problem and meet together to share concerns, problems, experiences, and ways of coping.

Caregivers support groups are part of a larger movement that the health care community calls the "self-help movement." Within the past ten years, many mental health professionals have come to realize that people under emotional stress don't always need professional help to solve their problems. Since the people who know the most about a problem are the ones who've been through it, they're quite capable of solving their own problems.

On my desk as I write this is a newsletter from my local hospital that lists support groups that it sponsors. Included are groups for those dealing with anorexia/bulimia, arthritis, bereavement, cancer, and strokes. Every week, my local newspaper lists support group meetings for families of crime victims, survivors of suicide, widows, and widowers.

Support groups are not another name for group therapy, and their leaders are not usually psychiatrists or psychologists. Groups that deal with health problems are often led by nurses. Mental health groups are often led by social workers.

A Christian support group is similar, but in addition, it draws on God's resources, which are infinitely greater than any human leader's. In my home county at present, besides Christian Caregivers, there are Christian Cancer, Christian

Widows, Christian Single Parents, and other support groups. It's a very practical way for Christians to "carry each other's burdens" (Galatians 6:2) and to discover the infinite riches of God's grace in a personal and practical way. The leaders of these groups are not experts who know all the answers, but people willing to struggle with you as you seek to be obedient to whatever God wants you to do.

Beware of any group, Christian or otherwise, that makes you feel guilty or inadequate or in any way adds to your burdens.

What should you expect from a support group?

▶ Accurate information about the common problem, whatever it may be. The way such information is shared may vary—from informal "talking it over" between leaders and participants to printed materials to speakers, films, and tapes.

▶ A supportive atmosphere with opportunities to share your story, to be listened to, and to listen to others without being judged, condemned, put down, or made to feel guilty for your feelings.

▶ Confidentiality. It's a basic rule in all self-help groups that all sharing is confidential.

▶ Leadership by example. Leaders should be warm, caring people who gently direct discussions without overcontrolling them.

▶ Acceptance. This should be a place where it's "okay to cry," but not a place with a "Gee, isn't it awful!" atmosphere. Honesty should be encouraged, yet at the same time, it should not be a "pity party."

▶ Availability of the leaders for consultation between meetings and encouragement to form friendly relationships with other group members (by an exchange of phone numbers, for example).

In addition, a Christian support group should be sensitive to participants' spiritual needs, give prayer support, and provide a ministry of encouragement.

Typically a Christian Caregivers Support Group member will say, "I didn't realize how badly I needed this until I got here."

But support groups are not for everyone. Some people are very successful at building their own informal support network to help them through the hard times. Others are not comfortable sharing with strangers and may need one-on-one counseling. Others may find that the makeup or procedures of a particular group are not right for them. You may need to try more than one group to find one you like (assuming that you live in a metropolitan area where you have such choices).

"THIS IS KILLING YOU"—HARRIET'S STORY

Harriet is a single, retired social worker whose mother came to live with her six years ago. This is her story:

"My life totally changed when I brought Mother to live with me. She'd been living near my brother and his wife [500 miles away], but she couldn't go on living by herself. When she got here, she was much more disoriented than I'd realized.

"I'd taken early retirement a few months before, intending to return to school and gear up for a second career. I thought I'd take about a year off to travel and consider my options. All that was off!

"It felt like having a child (even though I'd never had children). She was eighty-six, going on three. Mother couldn't be left alone, but she got real upset if I got a sitter. A friend would come and 'visit' her while I'd go out, and an old friend who'd done housework for me for years came to work two days a week. That was the only time I could either catch up on my sleep or go out.

"My brother and sister-in-law would come here three or four times a year and take her out. Then, boom, they were gone. And that was it. Mother had no other visitors. She didn't know anyone here. I finally got the church to send a visitor once a month, and the pastor came once a year to give her communion. Aside from that, I got no support from my church.

"A lot of my friends went away; they'd come over and visit once and never come back. It was like when I got divorced, and my friends all stayed away—I guess they thought I was contagious. I had to make a whole new group of friends.

"It was hard to find things for Mother to do. I fixed up my yard so she could do a little gardening from a wheelchair. Maybe if I'd had children, I would've been better at it . . . .

"My whole life was staying at home. That's what did me in. When I was a social worker, I could leave my problems behind at the office. I couldn't do that with my mother.

"Then I started to have health problems. I had a d. and c. My back started to go—I was in constant pain. My doctor finally told me, 'You have to do something. You can't go on like this—this is killing you.'"

About two years ago, Harriet put her mother in a nursing home where she made a very good adjustment. But that didn't make Harriet's guilt go away. However, good has come out of Harriet's suffering.

"The tremendous stress propelled me into therapy, which I'd never intended. I went into it out of desperation. But it's been a real growth experience. I found out that I'd never felt close to my mother or loved by her. I also discovered that I'd never really mourned my father's death. A lot of my work in therapy has been about grief and loss.

"I've started working as a volunteer for the rape crisis center, using my social work skills. As for the future, I still don't know. Go to work for a non-profit organization? Go back to school? I do know that I'm a much calmer and more accepting person as the result of all this."

BURIED ALIVE: KAREN'S STORY

Rather than talk in general about what a caregivers support group can do, I'd like to tell you the story of how Christian

Caregivers Support Group was used to help a particular caregiver.

Karen and her mother were both widows who'd always been close, so living together seemed the natural thing to do. What Karen had in mind when her mother moved into her home was something like television's "Golden Girls." But the reality turned out to be quite different.

Karen's mother, Hazel, had the beginnings of Parkinson's disease. Typically, its onset was slow, but as the disease progressed, Hazel found the ordinary tasks of housekeeping difficult, then impossible. Yet her true condition was hidden from outsiders.

"There came a time when she wasn't recognizing people," Karen said, "and she'd ask me, 'Who is that?' I would tell her and then she'd greet the person as if she knew him."

Her mother's growing helplessness forced Karen to make the decision to give up her job to take care of her mother. It would be hard financially, but she could manage with part-time work. Karen's job was so stressful that it left her without the energy to care for the household and her mother, so she was not leaving something she loved. But she was walking away one year short of having a vested retirement with the company. Like many women, Karen will face old age without a pension of her own.

When a neurologist finally diagnosed Hazel's Parkinson's disease, both women were very depressed.

"We're both people who like to know things," Karen said, "so we went to the library and took out two books on Parkinson's. Neither of us finished reading them; they were too depressing. So was the Parkinson's support group we went to. We could look at some of those people and see what was ahead for us."

After Christmas, Hazel began to slip rapidly and Karen, realizing that her mother could no longer be alone, shelved her plans to work part time.

The single caregiver is at great risk. There's nobody at home to give her emotional support and share the load. Over the years, single people build up networks of family, friends, and acquaintances. Suddenly, when they stay at home with a parent, these are all gone. The result can be a dangerous social isolation. This is what Karen started to experience.

When Karen's mother had moved in, Karen took her back to her mother's old church and did not go to her own.

"I lost the spiritual support I'd had before," Karen said. "I had also lost the uplifting strokes you get from other people at work. It was just mother and me. Her life became my life.

"I did get together with the family—I had my grandchild once a week, but my sons did not realize the full extent of what I was going through. Parkinson's is such a funny disease. Patients have good days and bad days. My family would see mother on a good day and think because she was doing something then that she always could. So they thought I was babying her.

"Getting any kind of meaningful respite was just too expensive. Occasionally, my mother would spend a week with my brother and his wife. The day after she'd leave, I'd feel like I'd been freed from a great burden. Then the day before she'd come back, I'd start dreading it!"

Parkinson's affects some patients' minds; as it progresses, patients become like Alzheimer's patients. As Hazel got worse, she no longer recognized Karen at times. She got up and began wandering at night.

"I knew I had to get to some kind of support group, someone in a similar situation to share with and to learn. That's when I saw the article on Christian Caregivers in the paper. I clipped it out, but it took me six months to even make the first phone call. I kept thinking, 'I don't need this. I can handle it.' I allowed myself to get way far down before I realized that I could not handle it."

Being isolated with a demented parent has been likened by another single caregiver to being "buried alive." You know there's a world out there, you know there's a God who cares, you know there may be other people who can help, but it's more than you can do to pick up the phone, admit you're hurting, and ask for help. This is especially true if, like Karen, you've been raised to keep all your emotions bottled up inside. Talking to "outsiders" about family matters is taboo. As one Christian caregiver said, "It doesn't feel right to be talking to you about my mother."

I remember Karen at her first support group meeting. She reminded me of someone frozen in stone. There was a human soul locked up in there, I was sure, but it was down so deep I didn't know how it would ever get out. For the first meeting, she said almost nothing. Then she called me and we talked for almost an hour. At the next meeting, I could see that a tremendous struggle was going on. Finally, she managed to get the words out and the dam burst.

That was only the beginning. Over the next few months, Karen's true self began to reemerge. She formed telephone friendships with others in the group. She sent encouraging cards and notes. Her prayers were beautiful. A deeply spiritual person had almost been buried before her time.

At the same time, Hazel's condition was steadily worsening. She had a series of little strokes, then a large one. Now Hazel could no longer hide her true condition from the world—it was laid bare for all to see. When the time came that Karen could no longer take care of her mother at home, she was given the grace to surrender her, first to a board-and-care home and then to a denominational nursing home located near her brother. Her brother is now the primary caregiver for their mother.

Letting go isn't easy, and for Karen, coming home to an empty house filled with her mother's things has caused her much anguish. But she's no longer the burned-out caregiver I first knew. She's now the person God intended her to be: compassionate, spiritually mature, and a great help and inspiration to others.

5

Deliverance from the Captivity of the Past

"The Spirit of the Lord is upon me, because he has chosen me to bring good news to the poor. He has sent me to proclaim liberty to the captives and recovery of sight to the blind, to set free the oppressed."
Luke 4:18, TEV

Almost all of us have unfinished business from the past with our families, but as long as we can keep parents and siblings at a distance, we can remain unaware of it. But if care-giving forces family members to interact closely, old feelings from childhood may suddenly rise up in all their former intensity.

Some caregivers are actually in captivity to the past. They are being controlled by events from their family histories that are thirty, forty, or fifty years old. If you find that you can't put into practice some of the suggestions in previous chapters—you can't set limits to your parent's demands or you can't accept her as she is now—you may need to be freed from some past influence that is oppressing you. Unless you allow the Lord to free you, you will not be able to take care of a parent in a healthy manner.

And you may find that not even death will free you from your parent's control.

LIKE MOTHER, LIKE DAUGHTER

Marilyn was a Christian woman in her fifties who was holding down two jobs while trying to build a private practice in counseling. Although she thought of herself as competent and self-reliant, she was sinking deeper and deeper into depression. It was taking at least two martinis a night just to keep her going. When she tried to cut down on her drinking, she found, to her horror, that she could not.

As her misery deepened, she withdrew into herself—friends and family complained that she was getting scatter-brained, always losing things. She tried self-improvement books; she saw a minister and a psychiatrist. Nothing helped. If anything, she was drinking even more. Until one night, when something happened.

"I was drained from my day's work. Idly, I sat toying with an empty cocktail glass, when suddenly, I began to be bom-barded by painful memories. My thoughts began to center around my mother, dead for twenty years.

"I'd always thought I resembled my dad, but that night, I was struck by how much my mother and I were alike. Everybody said we looked alike. She became depressed in midlife when her children left home. So did I (although I tried to fill the void with work). She tried to be very self-reliant and could never ask for help. Neither could I. She took medication and drank alcohol; I had been drinking martinis every night for ten years.

"My soul was flooded with fear. Was she an alcoholic? Could I be an alcoholic too?"

Marilyn ran to the phone to call a friend who was a recovering alcoholic. Following counseling at an alcohol rehabilitation clinic, Marilyn was steered toward Alcoholics Anonymous meetings, where she found loving support. Meanwhile, through daily confession and prayer, she was mending her relationship with God. But there was more to come.

"I was talking to Ron, a friend of mine who had a similar family history. He startled me when he said, 'Marilyn, you haven't yet buried your mother.' I realized at once that God was speaking to me through Ron.

"I made a list of all the fears and resentments I held against Mother and took them to a Christian counselor. I told them all, one by one, in detail. Suddenly, I found myself saying 'I don't know if my mother really loved me,' and crying like a baby."

All those years that Marilyn had denied being like her mother, she was actually walking the same path, drawn along in her mother's footsteps as if by an invisible cord. Like her mother, she had suppressed her fear and anger and numbed her hurts with alcohol. Now that Marilyn was able to open up all the hidden hurt places in her heart and let God in, she was finally freed from the control of the past. She was also now free to forgive her mother, a sick woman who had tried to do her best, and to remember her with love and compassion. She was healed.

ASK GOD TO SHOW YOU THE TRUTH

Do you still feel like a child when you're around your parents? Are they still relating to you as if you were twelve years old? This is a good indicator of trouble ahead. One research study of daughters caring for mothers revealed that the more "peer-like" (adult-to-adult) the mother/daughter relationship, the less stress the daughter experienced in caregiving. This confirms my own informal observation. Adult children who haven't been able to break free from their parents' control suffer a great deal as caregivers.

Many of these people have been fooling themselves for years, believing that they're free when they're not. Like Marilyn, they may not like the controlling parent. They may deny that they're at all like that parent. But the truth is quite different.

Heed the words of a caregiver named Laura, who found this out:

"My mother didn't have to say a word. All she had to do was put on her disapproving face, and even though I'm now fifty-two and she's eighty-eight, I was once more a fearful child. When I saw 'that face' as a child, I knew I was in for it, and I'd get a knot in my stomach and tiptoe around, trying not to set her off. Then she'd get on me, and I'd rage inwardly, powerless to stop her or to defend myself. I realize now that she was reducing me to this helpless rage in order to control me, but somehow knowing that didn't seem to help. I was really worried because I could see that whenever my daughter or daughter-in-law did something that reminded me of my mother, I felt uncontrollable rage—the rage of the small child still inside me. I asked God to show me if there was anything else I needed to do.

"When He did begin to show me the truth, it was very painful. He showed me that I was a lot like my mother!

"Early in life, I had decided I would never become like my mother. Her nagging and criticism drove me wild. She saw only the negative side of everything and continually dwelt on people's shortcomings and faults. . . . Wait a minute, I was dwelling only on *her* shortcomings and faults, and I always had! Just like my mother! I, too, had always found it easy to be critical and difficult to find words of praise. Just like my mother! My children complained that I had a certain tone of voice and a certain look on my face that I used on them. Just like my mother! I had raised my children with too much negativism and not nearly enough praise and affirmation. All the time that I had been denying that I was like my mother, I'd been acting like her.

"I took this insight that God had given me to a Christian counselor and began letting out some of my feelings. My biggest problem was what to do with my rage. I was really still too angry with my mother to forgive her—not on an intellectual level (I knew she'd had a dreadful childhood herself and she had done the best she could), but on an emotional level, where it really counts—and yet I knew that forgiveness was essential.

"The more I tried to forget some of these past incidents from my childhood, the more I thought about them. There were things I hadn't told my counselor—memories that to me were so painful and even shameful that I'd never told another living soul. It felt very disloyal to say anything—my mother had always impressed on me the importance of keeping family matters in the family. We didn't wash our dirty linen in public. But I was desperate.

"So I took these memories to my counselor and 'spilled the beans.' It was so cleansing. Some of these incidents seemed almost too petty to mention—like an unjust punishment, or the fact that she never liked any present I ever got her. But the emotion that came out with these memories was tremendous. I wept buckets.

"When it was all over, I was able to say 'I forgive you' for all of this and mean it. A tremendous weight was lifted from my shoulders. From then on, I was able to be with my mother without feeling all those old childish emotions. I'm sure that talking to my counselor saved my sanity. Mom never stopped being a put-down artist, but her snide remarks no longer bothered me. I consciously began looking for her good points and strengths rather than just focusing on her faults and weaknesses."

When the Son frees you, you are free indeed.

CONFRONTING A PARENT

Sometimes, counselors will recommend confronting a parent with your feelings. (This would not have worked in Laura's case because her mother simply refused to discuss the past.) What is confrontation? It's *not* a battle and it's not done in anger. It's going to a parent, looking her lovingly in the eye, and saying, "Mom, there are a few things you and I need to talk about." Then, without accusing, blaming, or reproaching, you tell her how you feel, especially how the way she treats you makes you feel. Use a sentence like "When you _____, I feel _____. I would really like us to have a better relationship."

But confrontation will not work if the parent has become mentally impaired. In that condition she is no longer capable of doing the work involved in repairing a relationship. The combination of a mentally impaired parent and an adult child still looking to this parent for the love and nurturing she never got in childhood can be deadly.

THE UNBLESSED CHILD

Ethel is a caregiver who had never felt close to her mother as a child. Like Marilyn, she preferred her father. After her father died, her mother continued to live in a distant city near Ethel's only sister. Her mother became ill, then was hospitalized. Without consulting Ethel, her sister put their mother in a nursing home. Ethel was irate.

The nursing home said her mother was mentally impaired. Nonsense, said Ethel, she's only a little depressed. She took her mother out of the nursing home and brought her back to her home to live.

Overnight, Ethel was plunged into the nightmare existence called "the thirty-six hour day." (The phrase also serves as the title of a book about Alzheimer's disease.) Ethel's mother had to be bathed, fed, dressed, and toileted. She was incontinent and had frequent "accidents." She slept poorly and began wandering so Ethel could not leave her alone for a moment, day or night. She competed with Ethel's husband and grown son for Ethel's attention. After a few months, both left, and Ethel's husband eventually divorced her.

Ethel lost all her friends; she was angry and bitter at her family, but she kept on. Even when a doctor insisted that her mother be placed in a nursing home for her own safety, Ethel resisted. When she was finally forced to place her mother in a nursing home, she visited every day and interfered in her mother's care. She simply could not let go.

A beautiful story of self-sacrifice? Not exactly. The clue to Ethel's behavior is contained in the following statement: "I was giving her what I wish I'd gotten from her as a child."

In mothering her mother, Ethel was really trying to mother herself. Denied her mother's tender love in childhood (her sister was the favored one), Ethel, once she got her mother in her clutches, was determined not to let go until she'd rewritten the past and made it come out right this time.

Why is this deadly?

"I used to fantasize about killing us both," Ethel said. "That's when I knew I was on the edge and needed help."

Ethel is an extreme example of the "unblessed child." As the Rev. Doug Manning explained in his book *When Love Gets Tough: The Nursing Home Decision*, one child is, for some reason, not the favorite. One or both parents withhold their approval. Some children will rebel from this, but others redouble their efforts to please their parents. When they perform in order to win love, they become the victims of the "no blessing equals control" pattern.

"As long as they are desperate for the blessing, they are controllable," Rev. Manning says. "Since control is the name of the game, the blessing can never be given and the child chases a carrot on a stick for the rest of his life."[1]

Often, in an effort to win approval at last, this unblessed child will become the parent's caregiver. At an unconscious level, she believes, "If I take care of Mom, she'll see how good I really am and finally, she'll love me best."

Instead, the dutiful child who does everything for the parent gets nothing but disapproval. When the favored child (who does little or nothing) visits, she's praised.

Nancy was one of the angriest caregivers I've ever met.

"Nothing I do seems to please my mother," she fumed. "She's giving away all her household things to my two brothers while I get nothing. Yet I do everything for her and they do nothing. What am I—her stepchild?"

Despite her anger, she dutifully complied with all her mother's requests, no matter how inconvenient.

"There's an easy, two-letter-word solution to your problem," I told her. "It's no."

Only Nancy held the key to this trap in which she was locked, but she couldn't seem to bring herself to use it. If she wasn't the unblessed child in the past, she was certainly getting the full, unblessed-child treatment from her mother right now.

Shortly after that conversation, Christian Caregivers Support Group held its third anniversary dinner and celebration. Our speaker was the Rev. Ned Holmgren. One of the things he suggested in his speech was gently touching the person receiving our care and saying, "God loves you."

Nancy reported back to us later that she'd tried it and a miracle happened. Her mother began telling her, "I don't know what I'd do without you; you're the only one who cares." Nancy's mother even began giving her daughter some of the possessions that Nancy had longed for but never had the courage to ask for.

If you are an unblessed child, your only hope of becoming free of your parent's control is to renounce all hope of getting her blessing. Otherwise, you'll remain in bondage. Instead of waiting for a blessing from her mother, Nancy gave up hope of getting it and blessed her instead. She acted instead of reacting. This change was not a permanent one. Nancy's mother once more became demanding and angry, but now Nancy was free.

THE NONCHRISTIAN PARENT

Christian caregivers can suffer a great deal of anguish if their parent is not a Christian. "What will become of her?" they ask. "Why doesn't God answer my prayers for her?"

It will be very difficult for you to lead a parent to Christ if you want something from her that was not given to you in childhood. She'll sense, at an unconscious level, that your attempt to help her is conditional: you give her love and approval in exchange for her conversion.

On the other hand, it's important not to give up hope. Somebody else may be able to help her spiritually, even if you can't. The most important thing you may be able to do is to let go.

"My mother never ceases to amaze me," said Elaine, a Dallas caregiver. "Since she came to live with us, she's started going to church. She hasn't been to church for over forty years—since my brother died. But after Dad's death, she was sort of looking for a way to return but she didn't know how. Living with us solved the problem. The first Sunday she was with us, she was all dressed and ready to go to church with us without my saying a word. You could have knocked me over with a feather!"

Sometimes, when the circumstances that held a parent back from accepting Christ are removed, the elder does a complete turnaround. For example, a parent might not have had the strength to oppose a strong-willed, domineering mate.

Marion was a widow whose parents were nonbelievers. Her mother was especially adamant. She threatened to leave her husband if he ever became "one of those damned religious fanatics." Marion explained what happened: "So he got cancer and she left him anyway! I guess she just didn't want to take care of him. They must have been really unhappy together all those years for her to feel that way, but I'm still having a hard time accepting this.

"Anyway, I took him in to live with me after his surgery and he died six months later in my home. But those were the most beautiful six months! He accepted the Lord and was as eager to learn about Him as a little child. Every day, we would have Bible study and prayer together. I could see him growing as a Christian right up to the end."

Even if your parent is hostile toward spiritual things and resists any attempt to lead her to the Lord, you can ask her permission to pray for her out loud, in her presence. Prayer that expresses sincere concern for your parent's welfare and asks for God's blessing for her will seldom be refused.

Occasionally, adult children are unpleasantly surprised when a parent who seemed to be a sincere Christian all her life turns into a scoffer. "Is this her infirmity talking and not her real self?" they ask. "Or was she wearing a mask before and this is now her true self?" It's hard to know, but don't give up hope. Turning away from God may be a reaction to her grieving and losses. Don't argue about religion. Instead, use the active listening techniques you learned in chapter 3 and pray. If allowed to talk out her feelings, your parent may rediscover God in an even deeper way.

ALLOW YOURSELF TO GRIEVE

If you must give up something—whether it's hope of getting a blessing from your parent or hope of being able to share Christ with her yourself—the natural reaction is grief. Allow yourself to grieve. Yes, grieving is painful, but hanging onto a false hope to avoid pain will prove even more painful in the long run. Hanging on will have an adverse effect on your mental health and stunt your spiritual growth.

Jesus tells us, "Blessed are those who mourn" (Matthew 5:4). The pain of grieving is intense but limited. If you allow yourself to mourn (grieve), you have God's assurance that you will be comforted, and when it's over, it's over. If you refuse to grieve, it will never be over.

SIBLING RIVALRY

When the feelings of brothers and sisters are positive, siblings are a wellspring of admiration, love, and affection to draw upon during the hard times in life. But when negative feelings dominate, then anger, jealousy, and resentment make a bad situation worse.

Unfortunately, say many who counsel the elderly, caregivers may feel more pain from their relationships with siblings than from their relationship with their parents.

In one university study of men and women between the ages of twenty-five and ninety-three, almost 75 percent reported feeling rivalry with their siblings. This rivalry began in their earliest years when they competed for their parents' love and attention. In most families, when the children grow up, this rivalry is forgotten. But it may never really have gone away; the test will come when and if middle-aged siblings must care for an aging parent. If the rivalry has never been resolved, it will resurface and interfere with their ability to plan for the parent's care.

Some parents encourage their children to compete for their attention in order to control them. Asking children who've been subjected to this treatment to agree on care for a parent is like asking Cain and Abel to cochair a peace conference.

Carol experienced this sort of rivalry. "I've just come from the hospital," she said angrily. "Mother's due to be discharged soon and can't go home to her own apartment. My sister thinks I should take her home to live with me.

"I know it looks very logical. Diane works and I don't; she's gone all day and I'm home. So I should be the one to do it.

"But the entire time I spent visiting Mother, she talked about Diane. Diane this and Diane that. How great she looks.

How well she's doing at her job. How much she's done for her even though she's busy. Diane brings her a few flowers and that's wonderful. I spend a whole day trying to arrange for home care and that's not even worth mentioning.

"This has been going on all my life. Diane was always the star of the family. I was the 'good, quiet one' who always did what she was told. I can't take it any more! Diane may not understand, but I simply have too much anger to take my mother in to live with me. And I won't let Diane bully or cajole me into doing it!"

At least Carol isn't fooling herself by thinking this is her chance to replace Diane as their mother's favorite. She has no illusions about the situation, but she has no peace either. What's sad is that Carol and Diane's mother may not even have realized what she was doing. The sisters, by hanging onto the rivalry of their youth, are missing an opportunity to become friends.

Come Together to Make Decisions

Plans for a parent's care work best if all the adult children are involved in making them. Often, however, one adult child, usually the one living closest to the parent, takes over care without consulting her siblings. If that occurs, the siblings may have little interest in helping to carry out a plan they had no say in formulating.

This can drive brothers and sisters apart. The caregiver feels like the "good guy"—always there, always giving—and begins to cast her siblings into the role of "bad guys." The caregiver's resentment against her siblings mounts. She's doing everything and they're doing nothing. Yet she may not realize how much her own actions are contributing to the situation she resents so much.

When a brother or sister calls, the caregiver may say things like, "Now don't upset Mother by talking about money." The unspoken, subtle message is "See who's in charge of Mother. I am. See what good care I take of her. I look out for all her best interests. You are very much in a secondary role and see that you stay there!"

The noncaregiving sibling may resent being told how to act and what to do. His remarks may really *be* criticism, fueled by resentment and jealousy. However, what is interpreted by the caregiver as criticism may simply be his attempt to have some input about the care of the parent. The siblings become locked into an unspoken negative struggle with each other that could have been avoided if they'd been able to sit down and communicate about their parent adult-to-adult. Then both could feel they're contributing.

The Uninvolved Brothers

Because daughters rather than sons have traditionally been the primary caregivers of the elderly, it's not at all unusual for the daughters to have responsibility for 100 percent of the care while the sons have zero. What the daughters may not realize is that they've accepted without question the stereotype that caregiving is "woman's work." In this, they are aided and abetted by their parents, especially the mothers.

If there are uninvolved sons, mothers will excuse them with remarks such as, "Poor Sam's so busy!" When they do the least little thing, Mom fusses over them and praises them, while daughter fumes. One busy daughter was even instructed by her elderly mother as to her "duty" to look after her uninvolved brothers—both of whom were over fifty, married, and grandfathers!

Usually, a mother has too much invested in her children not to ignore or excuse the uninvolved adult child. The caregiver's problem is with her sibling, not her parent. She has to be sure that his lack of involvement does not stem from her failure to communicate honestly to him the kind of help Mom needs or the fact that she expects him to contribute. Everybody, even those siblings not on the scene, can contribute something—whether it be money, respite for the caregiver, phone calls, or attention to the parent. The list is endless.

As Jan, a member of Christian Caregivers, once said: "My sister-in-law said to me, 'Bill really loves your mom, but he can't handle old age and illness!'"

Seldom does a sibling come right out and state his feelings this frankly, but there are people who are not strong enough emotionally to be involved in the care of an aging parent. Your sibling's inability to deal with your parent's old age is his problem; you'll just have to accept that and move on without him. The reason for this behavior lies deep within him or within his relationship with your parent, and you can't know what the reason is nor can you heal it. If he can't or won't grow up, you can't make him.

If you can realize that his inability to cope comes from weakness rather than viciousness, perhaps you can replace some of your anger with compassion. In any case, giving up your expectations will at least eliminate him as a source of frustration.

Guidelines for Caregivers and Siblings

Is there anything caregivers and siblings can do to make things easier for each other? Yes, if they are willing to change the way they relate to each other.

1) Communicate with each other. In many families, adult siblings are in the habit of communicating with each other indirectly, through a parent, usually the mother. Joan calls Mother to thank her for her birthday gift and says, "By the way, is Betty all right? I didn't even get a card from her." Mother then puts down the phone and immediately calls Betty to say, "Why didn't you send your sister a birthday card?"

If your parent has been in de facto control of your communication with siblings, it's time to throw off this control and take it over yourself. When Mom has a medical crisis and is in a hospital bed, unable to act as arbitrator, it's a little late for Joan and Betty to learn to talk directly to each other.

2) Caregivers, inform your siblings of what's going on with your parents without waiting for them to ask. Not doing so will not only give your siblings an excuse for remaining uninvolved but may also arouse suspicion that you have

something to hide. This is especially true when it comes to money matters. There should be no secrets.

3) Siblings of caregivers, offer help before it's asked for. Don't assume that because the caregiver doesn't ask, everything is under control. Caregivers are very hesitant to ask for help. Think of something specific you can do and do it.

4) Show appreciation for each other. Compliment the caregiver for the good job she's doing—she desperately needs that affirmation. Look for each other's strong points and express admiration for them. Siblings, like all other human beings, live up to others' expectations. Expect the worst from each other and that's what you're likely to get.

5) Refuse to remain locked into your outgrown childhood molds. The favorite child didn't ask to be favored; it wasn't her fault. If you were the favorite, your sibling can't help but feel pain; don't lord it over her or form a closed circle with your parent that shuts her out.

6) Without dredging up a lot of past hurts, tell your sibling how you really felt about him as a child. If he tells you what he felt, you may find you're both surprised. This could be the beginning of new openness and honesty between you.

Forgiveness Is the Key to Inner Peace
It isn't always possible to heal your relationship with a sibling. Willingness on your part is only the first step. Healing is also his responsibility. Your sibling may have become addicted to alcohol and be irresponsible. He may have married someone who is hostile to you and/or your parents. He may have embraced a philosophy of life that encourages him to put himself first.

You can't control his actions, but you can control yours. Just as in healing your relationship with your parents, the key to your inner peace is forgiveness. Unless you can forgive both parents and siblings, you may be left, after caregiving is over, with a bitter legacy. The experience can even make you a bitter and unhappy old person yourself.

But forgiveness is neither easy nor automatic. Many

Christians have trivialized forgiveness by assuming that it is. Some Christian writers and speakers take this attitude: "You're commanded by God to forgive. Now do it!" If this is your expectation, you may be feeling ashamed, frustrated, and defeated by your difficulties with forgiveness.

David W. Brewer, a Christian counselor in West Palm Beach, Florida, struggled personally with the problem of forgiving a parent. This is what he says:

> I've also been discouraged by the lack of effective teaching on forgiveness. I read books, listened to speakers, and attended seminars, only to feel defeated because everyone seemed to make forgiveness sound easy, guilty because I could not forgive the way Christ had forgiven me, and discouraged because no one seemed able to give me the key I needed to unlock my heart from the bitterness that held it captive.[2]

The Process of Forgiveness
Brewer's explanation of the reasons for our difficulties and the process we must go through is the clearest I've ever seen. First of all, God forgives and forgets instantaneously out of His divine nature (Jeremiah 31:34). But we are not like God. Our feelings of self-worth are fragile, and we feel threatened and damaged by injuries inflicted by other human beings. To forgive as Christ forgave us, Brewer says we must move through four stages:

> 1) *"Reaction."* An injury is inflicted and we react by withdrawing from the source of the pain.
> 2) *"Evaluation.* We reflect on what has happened" and arrive at a value judgment. We feel threatened and react with more pain and anger.
> 3) *"Decision."* We may decide to forgive, but our forgiveness may be false. There are two types of false forgiveness:
> ▶ "blind forgiveness" in which we "deny that anything

significant [has] happened." We may make ourselves
forget by burying the incident; we may keep busy (especially with "religious" activities) in order to distract
ourselves. The result of this is a superficial, surface
kind of Christian life.

▶ "expectant forgiveness" in which our forgiveness depends on whether the person to be forgiven acts in a
certain way. ("If he acts sorry, I'll forgive him," we
may say.) This gives the other person control over our
spiritual lives.

4) "Action"—true forgiveness. This involves "becoming
fully aware of how someone's offense has threatened
us," including experiencing the painful feelings associated with the offense, facing the part we are playing in
keeping the resentment alive, and repenting of our failure to be honest about our feelings and to depend on
God alone for our sense of self-worth.[3]

How will we know that we have truly forgiven someone?
When we can think of that person in full acknowledgment of
what he has done without feelings of pain and resentment,
honestly desiring the best for him.

The opportunity to forgive and to heal the hurts coming
from our past relationships with parents and siblings is one of
the special graces God gives us when we care for elderly
parents.

NOTES: 1. Doug Manning, When Love Gets Tough: The Nursing Home Decision
(Hereford, TX: In-Sight Books, 1983), page 65.
2. David W. Brewer, "Why Can't I Forgive?" Discipleship Journal, Issue
46, 1988, page 27.
3. Based on Brewer, pages 27-29.

6

Counting the Cost of Caregiving

Therefore a man leaves his father and his mother and cleaves to his wife, and they become one flesh.
Genesis 2:24, RSV

"For which of you, desiring to build a tower, does not first sit down and count the cost, whether he has enough to complete it?"
Luke 14:28, RSV

Every role that we take on in life has its costs, and caregiving is no exception. Seldom does a caregiver count the cost beforehand. Gradually, you may find yourself giving more and more care, until your caregiving is affecting the entire family, especially your spouse.

The first series of questions a married caregiver should ask is, "Do I have the wholehearted support of my spouse and children? Do they understand the sacrifices they may have to make, and are they willing to pull together as a family?"

What if your parents *and* your spouse's parents need care? How will you manage? How will the two of you agree to divide up your time and resources? Does your spouse have health problems, too? How much care will he require in the future, and how will your caregiving of parents affect his health?

Trying to balance the roles of wife, mother, grandmother, and caregiver is difficult. Your marriage vows require you to put your spouse first, yet your parent's needs can easily become overwhelming. Even with a spouse's support, caregiving is difficult. Without it, it's impossible.

If a marriage is strong, pulling together to care for a parent can make it stronger. If it's weak, caring for a parent could finish it.

I was asked at a seminar about the conflict between the needs of a parent and the needs of a spouse. I didn't have any pat answers for my questioner.

Finally, she said in exasperation, "It sounds like I may have to choose between my husband and my mother!"

"That's right," I replied.

There was a shocked silence. Obviously, she'd never thought it would come to that.

Life consists of hard choices and this is certainly one of them. You must count the cost before you begin. Are you willing to allow caregiving to cost you your marriage or your husband's health? Is early widowhood a price you'd be willing to pay? Few caregivers think in these terms, but this is the reality you may be facing.

AFTER GOD, YOUR SPOUSE COMES FIRST

One member of Christian Caregivers Support Group is trying to persuade a friend to come to our meetings. This friend (I'll call her Sarah) has virtually deserted her husband in order to take care of her mother.

Sarah's mother can no longer function independently, yet she refuses to leave her own home. Sarah and her husband have offered to take her mother into their home, but she refuses. So Sarah goes to her mother's house to help her daily, leaving her retired husband to fend for himself. She even stays overnight frequently. Her husband is lonely and miserable, but her excuse is, "What can I do? My mother won't move."

It's difficult to imagine a woman married almost forty years still acting like her mother's docile, obedient little girl. It's equally difficult to imagine a husband so nonassertive that he puts up with this. Even if they stay together, what kind of relationship will they be left with when the mother dies?

No married person should take on caregiving without the approval of her spouse. If approval is given, then it's necessary to work out in detail how far the spouse is willing to go. Does your spouse agree to inviting your parent to move in with you? Does he realize what this will entail? Have they gotten along well in the past? If not, there's no reason to think matters will improve in the future—relations in close quarters will probably be worse. Will care for your parent cost you your home's peace and tranquility? Are you both willing to pay this price?

Whether the parent lives with you or not, how much help can you expect from your spouse? Will you receive emotional support—i.e., a listening ear? Will he take over some of the extra errands and chores? If so, which ones? How far is he willing to go financially? Is the approval given reluctantly or grudgingly? If so, the message you're getting is "It's okay with me, but you're going to be doing it. Don't expect me to help and don't bother me with your problems. I don't really want to hear them."

If that is your spouse's attitude, going ahead with caregiving means you'll be essentially alone. You could end up just as lonely and isolated as a single caregiver. Unless you can build a support system apart from your spouse, you're placing yourself in jeopardy. Also, you will be a rare person if you do not resent your spouse's attitude. Caregiving under these circumstances will do nothing to strengthen your marriage and may place it at risk.

Plan for Time Alone Together
Time alone for husband and wife is an absolute necessity and should not be spent discussing the parent. Time for yourselves won't happen unless you carefully plan for it. Ironically, this may be harder to do if your spouse is supportive and enthusiastic about your taking on the caregiving role. He may not complain. He may not voice his own needs. I think this was true of my husband.

During the time I was seeing a counselor, I had a dream I've never had before or since. It ended with my husband bursting into tears and sobbing in my arms. Then I woke up. What did it mean? What was he crying about?

I took this dream as a warning from the Lord that my husband was feeling pain that he wouldn't consciously admit. I talked to him about our need to spend more time together and to give more attention to our marriage.

There are other, less dramatic, warning signs. Probably the most common is an outbreak of irritability and quarreling between two people who've previously gotten along very well.

Carla, a Florida caregiver, tells of her experience: "Jim's mother says things that upset me. She doesn't bother him, but I hold things in. Pressure builds up inside me and then I jump all over him."

This is almost to be expected when a parent needing care moves into your home. A couple's routine is upset, so there's an adjustment period to be gone through. The person receiving care requires patience, nerves are on edge, and the least little thing can set you off. You can't yell at the poor, helpless old person, but you can yell at each other. And you do. If this continues, the answer is not to blame each other but to realize that the irritability is a symptom of a larger problem that you need to work on together.

In Carla and Jim's case, they realized that they needed to get away from the house together regularly. Jim is retired, and before his mother moved in, they used to have a leisurely breakfast together and plan their day. Now, the minute they get up, Jim's mother is waiting for her breakfast. The solution for them was to leave after breakfast for a long walk together. This relaxes them and lets them deal with the pressures before they build up too much.

To deal with negative feelings and stresses, the two of you need positive experiences together that will strengthen your relationship. Some caregivers whose parents live with them are unable to leave their loved one alone to attend worship with their families. Sometimes they take turns—one attending while the other stays home. But this is no substitute for taking spiritual nourishment together. However, attending a Bible study, or some other small group fellowship will not only enable you to get out together but will also enable you to grow closer spiritually.

One of the costs of caregiving can be the financial cost of hiring someone to come in so you can get out with your spouse. If family members or friends offer to help give you respite, accept graciously. One caregiver's daughter, as a gift to her parents, offered to stay with her grandmother one weekend a month. If you have no family nearby who can give you this relief and you can't afford to hire help, you can ask your church for help. This is a service that most churches should be able to provide, and more would probably do so if the need were presented to them.

My husband and I were fortunate enough to be able to afford hired help, but even so, finding someone reliable and working out all the arrangements were major problems. We got away for weekends three or four times a year if possible, and for a week's vacation every year. It was expensive but worth it.

My mother did not like being left with a "sitter," as if she were a child. Few elderly parents do. But when I talked to her, she understood that it was only fair not to deprive my husband of my companionship. My concern about his needs and the health of my marriage helped to give me the strength to be firm with her about this. Also, it's important to find someone your parent likes to stay with her. After a while, my mother came to welcome the sitter as a change from her usual routine. She had almost no visitors and this was like receiving a visit from a friend.

My husband and I also got away individually. He went backpacking with his hiking buddies and was more than willing to stay with my mother for a weekend while I attended a professional conference or visited an out-of-town friend. But it was the time together that was so precious because it was so scarce. It felt as if we were stealing away together—and we were. When the time came to return, I felt like Cinderella after the ball.

THE CARE OF IN-LAWS

In many families the wife keeps up a relationship with both her parents and her in-laws while her husband, the in-laws' son, is often a bystander. If this is your situation, it's better to try to change it before heavy caregiving is needed.

"I take care of my parents in their own apartment, which takes a lot of time and energy. But in addition, I've always been the one who kept up a relationship with Tom's parents," Phyllis said. "I wrote, I sent cards, I phoned. That's a fairly common pattern in my generation. If this kept on, I didn't know if I could take care of both sets of parents. Then I thought, 'Why should I? These are his parents.'

"I decided I'd been wrong all these years. By doing it all, I'd made it too easy for Tom not to learn to communicate with his parents. So I stopped writing to his parents regularly, and when they called, I stepped aside and let Tom talk to them. At first he objected. But I told him that since they were his parents, I would no longer have the relationship with them for him. He was going to have to learn to do it. I'm always cordial with them—they're lovely people—but it's their son they need, not me."

If a parent moves into your home, you will have an instant in-law triangle. For a marriage to survive, it's necessary for the caregiving spouse to deal firmly with his or her own parent. It's unfair to expect your spouse to stand up to an in-law; not to be on your spouse's team will erode your marriage relationship in a hurry. If your parent attacks your spouse, you must defend him or her (courteously, of course). If your parent makes unreasonable demands of your spouse, you must be the one who sets limits.

It's especially important for the husband to assert his authority as the head of the house if a strong-willed parent comes into your home. If the parent is a mother, her generation may be more likely to recognize male authority in the home. Or, as one caregiver put it, "They'll try things with other women that they won't try with a man!"

Sometimes, the person receiving care will attempt (usually unconsciously) to form an alliance with one of the marital partners. It may be her own child; less frequently, it's the in-law. It's important for you and your spouse to see through these "divide and conquer" tactics. My mother, for example, developed a great fondness for my husband, who was very kind to her. But I soon realized that when my husband and I disagreed, she jumped in—on his side! So we tried to do our arguing out of her earshot.

The feeling that a spouse is not on your side can really hurt. Your spouse may not see the uglier side of your parent's personality—she may display it only when he's not around. One caregiver who complained to her husband about something her mother was doing was told, "Your mother is a wonderful woman! How could you say that?" When my husband said something similar, I replied, "Please—I don't need you to tell me what to feel. I just need you to listen." But I also realized that I shouldn't overdo the complaining; a spouse will soon grow weary of hearing it. I needed to find people other than my husband who would listen to me.

THE "RETIRED" CAREGIVER

If a caregiving couple is retired, they may have to postpone or cancel plans they had previously made. One husband who gladly invited his mother-in-law to move in was very content with the situation until he retired. Unfortunately, his retirement coincided with a worsening of his mother-in-law's health, and he found his activities greatly curtailed. He had difficulty accepting the reality of this. He would talk to his wife about going on long trips. She'd agree that they would go, knowing that it was impossible. He was not ready to face this and began to have stress-related health problems.

A caregiving son of retirement age had to leave his wife, whose health was poor, alone at home while he drove hundreds of miles to handle his mother's affairs. His wife never complained, but he was torn by guilt.

When things like this happen, caregivers (who might cheerfully sacrifice their own health) begin to ask themselves, "Is it right and fair to ask my spouse to sacrifice his health for my parent?"

Questions like this, and the conflicts and guilt they induce, are some of the stresses that drive married caregivers to counselors and support groups. There are no right or wrong answers, but if you share your hurts with other Christians, they can help to support you as you struggle with questions about relationships, not only with your spouse but also with children and grandchildren.

SECOND MARRIAGES, STEPCHILDREN, AND CHILDREN

Modern caregiving of the elderly is greatly complicated by divorce, remarriage, and stepfamily relationships. Perhaps your second husband, if you have one, hardly knows your mother. Is he going to be willing to share you with her? Also, your parents are not his children's grandparents. His children may have no affectional ties to them and resent the time, energy, and money the two of you spend on them. What then? This whole new area of family life has the potential for increased conflict.

It's certain, however, that a couple's caregiving will either be greatly aided or greatly hindered by the attitudes and actions of their children and stepchildren, whether these children still live at home or are adults who've left the nest.

You've probably heard the slightly cynical comment, "Grandparents and grandchildren are natural generational allies—they have a common enemy." There's a certain element of truth to this, but only if the affectional ties between grandparents and grandchildren have been established in early childhood. Children who grow up with grandparents who love them certainly learn respect for age, kindness, and compassion for the elderly. This is beneficial for children.

But it's not the same for them when a grandparent they hardly know, who has shown them little or no attention, or whose personality has been changed by illness is introduced into the home. The elderly suffering from dementia can become violent or behave in sexually inappropriate ways that children need to be protected from.

"I have very ugly childhood memories of my grandfather chasing my mother around the kitchen table with a knife," says Diana, a young mother in her thirties. Her parents kept her demented grandfather at home long after he should have been institutionalized.

GRANDPARENTS AND GRANDCHILDREN AS RIVALS

If you have children living at home, you must take into account the cost to them of your caregiving role. Talk to your children, especially if they're still living at home, about their feelings. Despite the possible benefits, they, too, will have adjustments to make. What will the cost be to them? Will they feel displaced or abandoned?

Alice, an Iowa caregiver, said, "My youngest child was still at home when my dad died and my mother moved in with us. He was thirteen, and since the older kids had left for college, he was like an only child. Suddenly, he had an eighty-one-year-old sibling competing for my attention, criticizing him for every move he made, and tattling to me about him. It was awful!"

This type of rivalry is very common. A dependent parent feels helpless and reverts to the tactics she used in childhood. In some cases, the rivalry is not with her grandchildren but with her great-grandchildren.

"My mother enjoyed my grandchildren unless I took care of them for the day or overnight," said June, an Oklahoma caregiver. "Then she resented them. My daughter and her husband really needed help. One of their children had open heart surgery when she was seven months old, and I took care of her older sister while she was in the hospital. My mother was snappish and put out the whole time she was here. My children offered to stay with my mother so my husband and I could get away, but I never accepted their offers because they'd have to bring the grandchildren here. My mother disliked them so much, it just wasn't worth it."

It's very difficult for your children to be kind and loving to your parent when they're cast into the role of rivals. It might help if you talk to them, explain what's going on, and enlist their aid in helping Grandma feel more secure so she doesn't have to compete for your attention. If they say, "I love you, Grandma," and if they pay attention to her, she may respond. At the same time, you need to be firm with your parent. Make it plain that you expect her to treat your children and grandchildren courteously. Then hope and pray. But don't give in and allow her to drive them away.

Children differ greatly in personality and maturity; you can't force them to love your parent. You may find that they are not strong enough emotionally to watch a beloved grandparent deteriorating, and they may practice denial or just withdraw. You can pray for them, but you can't change them. Their inability to deal with your parent's old age is their problem, not yours.

Reaping What We Sow

It became very clear to me, as I talked to families, that elderly grandparents tend to reap what they have sown. If they have sown love and attention in the grandchild's early years, they tend to reap the rewards of loving-kindness from grand-children in their old age. This was certainly true in families where grandchildren were happy to stay with Grandma or Grandpa in order to give their caregiving parents some respite.

There is often a "favorite grandchild" who can get Granny to cooperate when nobody else can. He or she is a blessing to the family—very useful but also very unfair to other grandchildren.

"I have one son who's a ray of sunshine when he visits my mother. He can josh her and she loves it. If the other son tries it, she flares up at him. I know this has hurt him," said Millie, a Texas caregiver.

Sometimes favoritism is obvious, and painful to watch. You can't help feeling hurt if your parent hurts your child. Perhaps your parent concealed her feelings successfully when she was younger but now no longer bothers to do so. When that happens, there's not much you can do.

At the opposite extreme, I've heard caregivers make statements like the following: "My children never visit my mother in the nursing home. I'm afraid they don't have any happy memories of her. She wasn't a very warm grandmother." "My brother wouldn't visit my parents for the entire time they had my grandmother living with them. He hated her." "My daughter hated to come home for visits when my mother was living with us because there was so much tension. She felt caught in the middle between her mother and grandmother, as if she were being asked to choose sides."

Your adult children may follow the very human tendency to take sides and make judgments that may or may not be fair. On the one hand are children who think their caregiving parent is doing too much. "You spoil Grandma rotten," said one adult child. "I certainly hope you don't expect me to care for you like this."

On the other hand, some children think their caregiving parent isn't doing enough. When Gertrude had to place her mother-in-law in a nursing home because she and her husband could no longer care for her at home, her adult daughter stopped speaking to her. They've been estranged ever since.

So, while adult children can be a great source of help and encouragement, they can also be a source of stress. The caregiver is pressured from both sides as she tries to meet the expectations not only of her parent but of her children.

And what of her own old age? She may have little time, while caught up in the responsibilities of caregiving, to build the ties with her own grandchildren that will help to support her emotionally in the future. This raises the question that every caregiver must answer for himself or herself: "If the cost of caregiving includes estrangement from my own children and grandchildren, am I willing to pay this price?"

I wish I had easy answers to all these questions. Caregiving is a balancing act, and every family is different. Nobody can decide for you. As you struggle with the effect of caregiving on relationships within the family, remember that God is the source of the wisdom that you will need, and He has promised to give it to you if you ask for it (James 1:5). Seeking God's guidance and struggling with these problems will stretch you and test you.

Sometimes the stress of caring for a parent will force you to deal with family issues that, in the past, you swept under the rug. While this is painful in the short run, in the long run you will become a wiser, more compassionate, and more loving person.

7

Love and Money
"Put your house in order."
2 Kings 20:1

Money is frequently cause for anxiety in caregivers and their families. You may wonder, "Does my parent have enough money to take care of her needs for the remainder of her life? How long will that be? How much is enough? What about medical care, and nursing home bills, if necessary? Will we need to help financially sometime in the future?"

These are all reasonable concerns, but they're seldom brought out in the open between adult children and their parents. Your parents may always have been very private about their finances. The spoken or unspoken message you may be getting is "It's none of your business!" Adult children may feel that if they bring up the subject, their parents will think they're waiting for them to die so they can get hold of their money.

It's hard to separate money and love. In the parable of the prodigal son, the son who stayed at home was angry because his father had given his brother his inheritance and then welcomed him home after he'd squandered it. What's more, the father spent money to give his brother a party. "He never gave me a party," the other son thought. "He must love my brother best. Spending the money on him proves it!"

Despite these concerns, both adult children and their parents need to talk about money. The time to do this is before the parent needs a great deal of care. The grim reality is that while people are living longer today, the costs of care are rising all the time. If you have to take over care of your parent, then the amount of money she has available does become your business. It will determine where she can afford to live and how much she can spend on services that may keep her out of a nursing home as long as possible.

You may find that, as your parent ages, she becomes tighter with money and more secretive. Old people don't become that way because they're aging but because they're afraid their money may be gone before they are. More than anything, most elderly people fear becoming a financial burden to their children.

In most states, adult children cannot be held legally responsible for a parent's care. But most adult children feel a moral obligation to help financially. They must answer difficult questions: How much will be needed? Should they take money set aside to educate children and use it for their parent's care? If they spend all their money on their parent's care, how can they provide for their own old age?

CARE VERSUS PRESERVING AN ESTATE

There are no easy answers to any of these questions. But it would be helpful if members of the older generation could let their children know where they stand financially. Then perhaps both generations might be able to agree that their first priority should be caring for the elders' needs in old age and not handing down an estate.

For many older people, it's a matter of pride to have an estate, no matter how small, to pass on to their children. They will scrimp and save and deny themselves; often, they will refuse to hire help they need in order to remain in their homes, thus hastening the day when they may need nursing home care.

Many elderly people have done this, only to find, when they had to enter a nursing home, that the costs soon used up all their savings anyway. At an average annual cost of $22,000 per year, a few years in a nursing home will reduce all but the extremely wealthy to paupers.

It's important for adult children to reassure their parents that in these times, when medical costs can be so ruinous, their parents' first priority should be to take care of themselves. If possible, all adult children in the family should agree to this goal. A family feud can erupt when one child wants the parents to spend money on their own care and another wants to save the money to preserve the estate.

But when the need for care is upon your parents, it's too late for them to make long-range financial plans. Even if your parents are still well and healthy now, you need to talk to them about finances.

"PUT YOUR HOUSE IN ORDER"

How should you approach your parents about financial matters?

One way might be to urge them to put their house in order (2 Kings 20:1). You might say something like this:

"You know, Dad (or Mom), we love you and we hope you'll be with us for many more years. But there are no certainties in this life, and nobody knows when the Lord will call you home. We've known too many people whose parents died and left behind a financial mess for them to straighten out. It would be very hard, when we're emotionally upset from your death, to try to figure out your finances, in addition to everything else we'll have to go through. We hope that you'll want to spare us that. Now, while you're healthy and your mind is sound, is the time to make some plans and put your financial affairs in order."

They may not agree immediately. It's a big step for them to contemplate their own possible future inability to care for themselves. Some who won't listen to their children are convinced by a lecture at a senior center given by a lawyer or financial planner, or by an article in a retirement magazine. (You might tactfully arrange for them to go to such a lecture or leave pertinent articles lying around.)

The Need for Estate Planning

What must your parents do to put their house in order?

Your parents need to know their assets, namely, the current value of their home and what their equity in it is worth, plus the worth of savings accounts, stocks and bonds, insurance policies, and any other possessions. A list of their assets, as well as other important information, should be kept in a *Personal Record File* (in addition to a safety deposit box), where it will be immediately accessible when needed.

The following checklist is reprinted by permission from *Estates: Planning Ahead*, Northern California Cancer Program, 1301 Shoreway Rd., Ste. 425, Belmont CA 94002:

Personal Record File
You can be very helpful to your spouse and other survivors by simply assembling in one place copies of certain records and documents that they will need.

A manila envelope, marked to show its contents and kept in a place known to your survivors, is sufficient. Only photocopies of important documents should be placed in this envelope. Originals should be safeguarded in a fire-proof place such as a safe-deposit box. Place a check mark (✔) in front of each item that you have enclosed and then enclose this list with the documents.

_____ (a) Will, with name and address of attorney.

_____ (b) Life, medical, property, and auto insurance policies, with name and address of insurance agent(s).

_____ (c) Real estate deed, title policies, closing statements, mortgages, record of mortgage payments, tax receipts, receipts for improvements over the years, etc.

_____ (d) Leases.

_____ (e) Name and address of broker or the stock certificates and bonds you own (plus the purchase slips or other records of cost and date of purchase), and exact registration or ownership if it is not evident from the enclosures.

_____ (f) Names of banks and savings and loans and account numbers, the names of bank or savings and loans officers with whom you deal, and exact registration or ownership.

_____ (g) List of other assets and locations (including loans, deeds of trust, and accounts receivable).

_____ (h) Safe-deposit box key, name and location of bank, and box number.

_____ (i) Income tax returns for the last three years,

plus name and address of persons preparing these returns.

_____ (j) Birth certificates for yourself, your spouse, and your dependents.

_____ (k) Marriage certificate or proof of divorce, if appropriate.

_____ (l) Automobile ownership certificate and registration receipt.

_____ (m) Social security card or record of number.

_____ (n) Veteran's discharge paper or certificate.

_____ (o) Contract(s) to which you are a party (including installment purchase agreements).

_____ (p) Business records.

_____ (q) Charge account numbers and plates.

_____ (r) Receipts, appraisals, or valuations for items of substantial value such as jewelry, furs, furniture, silver, art objects, antiques, etc.

_____ (s) List of close relatives, addresses and telephone numbers.

_____ (t) Funeral or memorial instructions, including names of your funeral director or memorial society.

_____ (u) General instructions to surviving spouse or children, including a list of advisors.

This personal record file will also be very helpful if you see an attorney or other advisors.

Your parents need a will, and you need to know where it is so that you can find it when the time comes. (Do not place it in their safety deposit box, which, in most states, is sealed immediately upon death.) In some states, a simple will can be made by filling out a form and having it witnessed and notarized. Low-cost legal help can often be found through your local Area Agency on Aging. A larger estate and a more complicated will require more extensive legal advice, preferably from an attorney who specializes in estate planning.

If you are named as executor of your parent's will, what will your duties be? The following list should be helpful to you.

▶In cooperation with your parent's attorney, find and read the will, notify the heirs, and have the will probated, if necessary.

▶Take possession of your parent's records and papers, collect valuables for safekeeping, take charge of personal property, arrange for necessary insurance coverage.

▶Take charge of all assets—remove and inventory the contents of the safety deposit box; transfer cash in bank accounts; reregister securities; inventory household and personal effects; collect on life insurance policies; take possession of all real estate records and arrange for management or sale; collect debts owed to estate.

▶Inventory and appraise all assets.

▶Arrange to liquidate assets to raise whatever cash is needed to pay fees, taxes, legacies to heirs, etc.

▶Analyze and review securities portfolio.

▶Distribute or sell personal and household effects in accordance with the provisions of the will.

▶Pay funeral expenses, taxes, claims, and bills.

▶File state and federal income tax returns.

▶Pay state and federal estate taxes.

▶Distribute the legacies to the heirs.

▶Prepare detailed report and accounting.

In addition to legal assistance, executors may require the expert advice and guidance of accountants, financial planners, and other professionals. The larger and more complex the estate, and the more complicated the will, the more difficult the executor's task becomes. If you know that your parent plans to name you as executor and that the estate is a complicated one, you should encourage him to let you get acquainted with the details of his financial affairs in advance. It will make your task that much easier.

In California, if the total value of your parents' estate is less than $60,000, it will not be subject to *probate*. (Probate codes differ by state.) The heirs can claim property merely by presenting a declaration form with attached copies of the death certificate and will to a bank, a transfer agent for stock, or other holders of assets.

While $60,000 may sound like a great deal of money, your parents may find when they add up their assets that their estate is worth more than they thought. The value of the equity in their home may be more than $60,000.

If an estate is over $60,000 and subject to probate, the fees for filing vary by state, but usually are a sliding percentage of the value of the estate. To preserve as many of the assets of their estate as possible, your parents can take steps now to avoid probate and to minimize inheritance taxes. The chief means for doing this is the *living trust*, also known as a *revocable trust*.

WHAT IS A LIVING TRUST?

A living trust is a legal arrangement by which a person's property is held and administered by a trustee for the benefit of another. These can be the same person; that is, your parent could be both the trustee and the beneficiary of a living trust.

Your parent could also name someone else—one of his children, a bank, a lawyer—as his trustee, either now or at some future time, to take effect if he should become incapacitated. A living trust is not always the most advantageous arrangement. An attorney would need to explain the pros and cons of their particular circumstances to your parents.

If they decide on a living trust, all assets must be transferred to the trust while the owner is alive and mentally capable of signing the papers. The task of making the transfers—which include the titles to all real property, bank accounts, stocks and bonds owned, etc.—can be time-consuming. (Details will vary according to state law, so any general statements you see about living trusts in a book or publication intended for a national readership may not apply in your particular state.)

Reducing Taxes After Death

The living trust is sometimes used to reduce estate taxes. Estates of more than $600,000 for a single person and $1.2 million for a couple are subject to federal estate taxes. The marital deduction is wasted if the property goes directly to the surviving spouse, but not if it's in a living trust. At the death of the first spouse, the trust is divided. The dead person's share of the assets goes into the trust, and the trust's assets are not included in the surviving spouse's estate. If the estate is large, the surviving spouse can keep more money for future care.

How about having your parent give away money or property now, before his or her death, to save on taxes? This is certainly a possibility, and there are many advantages to making advance gifts to charitable and religious organizations. However, gifts to family members may be subject to federal gift taxes. Your parent will need professional legal and financial advice before making a decision.

Who Should Be the Trustee?

The duties of a trustee are similar to those of the executor of an estate given earlier. There is considerable paperwork. If there are large assets, a trustee needs to understand investments and their management or seek financial counseling.

If your parent is unable to administer the trust himself, who should do this? Obviously, it should be someone that he trusts. If it's an adult child, it must be one who has the ability and time to do the work and whom siblings and other family members trust. Fees for secretarial or accounting assistance to administer the trust can be charged to the trust. If your parents name a third party as the trustee—a bank or a lawyer—fees for administering the trust can be considerable.

Should siblings share the responsibility? Legal experts say no. The requirement that two people sign the document before any action can be taken could lead to costly delays, especially if the two trustees live at any distance from each other. Having two trustees increases the risk that they might be unable to agree to take necessary action on behalf of the trust (for example, if it should become necessary to sell a piece of real estate in order to pay medical bills). However, establishing one person as trustee can lead to hard feelings among siblings. ("Why did you pick him? Why not me?")

To avoid future enmity, one elderly man was going to appoint his two sons, who didn't get along very well, to be cotrustees. "If they can't agree now," his lawyer advised, "what makes you think they're going to be able to agree any better in the future—especially when money is at stake?"

THE ELDERLY AS FINANCIAL VICTIMS

It's sad but true that the elderly are frequently targeted as victims of fraud. Every winter in Florida, certain criminal families move through the state, offering cheap "repairs" to elderly people living on tiny incomes. Their specialties are paint that washes off with the first rain, "new" roofs that still leak, and "new" driveways that crack and split. But by the time the fraud is discovered, the criminals have moved on to their next victims.

Trusting elders have been sold thousands of dollars worth of health insurance they don't need and dance lessons they'll never use, not to mention all the "sure thing" investments that turn out to be risky or fraudulent, depriving the elderly victims of their life savings. It may be difficult to protect your parents from this kind of exploitation.

Few elderly people will check out purchases and investments with their children before making them—in most families, financial advice always flowed the other way. But your parents might be willing to listen to tactfully worded warnings; e.g., "Mom, did you hear about the latest scam? It seems this widow got a phone call . . ." or, "Did you know what can happen if you give out your credit card number over the phone? Listen to this. . . . "

The unexplained disappearance of money may be the first indication that a parent is slipping mentally. You'll need to talk to your parent about it (tactfully, of course). An elderly man living alone in Florida became an alcoholic after his wife's death. A neighbor who "befriended" him took control of his checking account, milking it for sums of money when he was too drunk to know what he was doing. Another neighbor alerted members of his family, and they were able to put a stop to the theft before his money was all gone.

When things like this happen, an elderly parent may realize he needs protection and agree to have an adult child sign on his checkbook and take over bill-paying. But even this may not go far enough.

Many families are reluctant to believe that an elderly relative is mentally incompetent when indeed he is. When her father's attorney called Jane to warn her that her father was getting confused and would be a "sitting duck" for unscrupulous people, Jane was skeptical. He seemed fine to her. Yet within a few months, neighbors had persuaded him to switch to their attorney and write them into a new will.

"I tell this story so that others will realize that there are people who will take advantage of the vulnerable elderly," Jane said. "Now I realize that his attorney was acting out of friendship. But these people who tricked him had been his neighbors for thirty years! How could anyone do this?"

By the time her father's doctor told Jane she'd have to petition a court for conservatorship, it was too late for her father to protect himself by giving her *durable power of attorney.*

It's the rare parent who says, as Ron's father did, "Son, I may not always be as sharp as I am now and somebody might take advantage of me and try to get my money. If that happens, I'd want you to act for me, so let's see about setting up a durable power of attorney for you. Then, it'll be there if we ever need it."

DURABLE POWER OF ATTORNEY

A simple power of attorney is a legal arrangement giving one person the authority to act for another—i.e., to transfer property, pay bills, etc. But when the mental competence of the one granting power of attorney ends, so does the power of attorney. Durable power of attorney, however, is granted by your parents when they are mentally competent and continues (endures) even if their mental competence ends.

Think of the durable power of attorney as a form of insurance for your parents—if anything happens to them, the person they have chosen in advance would act on their behalf. If they never become incapacitated, it would never be used. (Durable power of attorney is for financial matters, although some states permit it for health care; see chapter 10.)

If a parent becomes mentally incapacitated and there is no durable power of attorney, a number of unpleasant things can happen. Relatives might not be able to agree on a course of action. The state might have to step in and appoint a legal guardian for your parent. Or, to protect your parent's assets, you might have to petition a court to have a guardian appointed. This is a painful procedure for an adult child and humiliating for the parent who stands to lose all his legal rights. In most cases, a durable power of attorney, executed before he becomes incapacitated, avoids this. (However, to place a mentally-impaired relative in a nursing home against his will, you may still have to be appointed guardian by a court.)

A durable power of attorney need not be given only to family members. In Tempe, Arizona, a retirement community's residents formed "Concerned Friends," which contracts with people to make decisions for them if they become incapacitated. The instrument used is the durable power of attorney. The decisions and the handling of the monies are overseen by a board of directors. When there is no close family or when families are far away geographically or divided by mistrust, this may be a possible solution.

THE GUARDIANSHIP PROCESS

Between 300,000 and 400,000 people were under guardianship in the United States in 1987, according to an investigation by the Associated Press. They cannot marry, divorce, vote, receive money, hire an attorney, or enter into any legal agreements. Court-appointed guardians have the power to decide where they will live, how they will be fed and clothed, who will be permitted to visit them, and what medical treatments and procedures they will receive.

This is enormous power for one person to have over another, and like any power, it can be abused. In some courts, guardianship hearings tend to be a rubber stamp procedure. Over 40 percent of the elderly in guardianship court cases were not represented by an attorney, and 49 percent were not present at their hearings. After appointing a guardian, many courts do not have the resources to supervise the arrangement very closely. A guardian can charge excessive expenses to a ward's estate and, in some jurisdictions, go unchallenged. Guardians have stolen from their wards' estates and been caught, but often only after most of the assets were gone.

Guardianship proceedings can be filed not only by family members but by nursing homes, hospitals, and social workers for welfare agencies. If an elderly person has no relatives (or none willing to take over), he may become a ward of a public guardian who deals with hundreds of cases. In some locales, private "professional guardians" sometimes take over when there's no family. A private foundation in my county is the appointed guardian of some of our more affluent elderly people.

Once their legal rights have been taken away by a court of law, it's difficult for the elderly person to get them back. When Amanda White lay in a nursing home in a coma, her daughter successfully petitioned a court to declare her mother incompetent and appoint herself guardian. But when Amanda unexpectedly recovered, she found that courts don't automatically reverse themselves. Amanda had to get statements from the psychiatrist, doctor, and minister who'd signed the original guardianship petition, then petition the probate court for a hearing. It took her a full year and hundreds of dollars in legal fees to win back her rights.

It isn't easy to decide if and when you should try to have a parent declared incompetent. How strong is the evidence of her mental incapacity? (Mere eccentricity is not the same as incompetence, nor is merely ignoring your good financial advice.) Will this cause estrangement between you and your parent? Is the money worth it? My opinion is that you should be very slow to institute incompetency proceedings, and then only as a last resort.

What does a guardian do? The laws of each state spell these duties out in considerable detail. If you become guardian for your parent, you will have to perform time-consuming duties, keep careful records, and file reports that are mandated by the court. If your parent has investments, you must manage them prudently. This requires the same diligence and financial expertise as management of a trust's property.

If one of your parents has Alzheimer's disease and you can foresee mental incapacity ahead, urge your other parent to get legal advice at once. Since assets must be transferred thirty months before entering a nursing home to qualify for Medicaid assistance, the sooner they're transferred to the surviving partner, the better. (For help in doing this, see the Alzheimer's disease resources listed in the Appendix for chapter 10.) Also, in order to avoid competency hearings and guardianship, transfer must be done while your parent still has the mental capacity to sign the papers.

ACT BEFORE IT'S TOO LATE

If your parent plans to grant durable power of attorney or set up a living trust, he must do so before some crisis (such as a stroke) makes it impossible. A physical impairment will not make it legally impossible for him to sign the papers, nor will a mental impairment in which he has good days and bad days. The legal requirement is that he understand the significance of the act of signing at the time he performs it. On his lucid days, he can sign legally binding documents. But it's dangerous to delay; you never know when it may become too late to take the legally necessary steps to protect your parent's assets.

Financial matters can be one of the most complex, difficult, and time-consuming duties of the caregiver. The key to performing these duties well is really the attitudes of those who have the money and those who must manage it for them. "Put your house in order" refers to more than just a financial house. *House* also means family.

From time immemorial, siblings have battled each other for their parents' money and possessions. We need look no further than the Old Testament kings and their children for horrible examples of this. These siblings stopped at nothing, including murder.

James spoke of the reasons for this when he wrote, "Where there is jealousy and selfishness, there is also disorder and every kind of evil. . . . Where do all the fights and quarrels among you come from? They come from your desires for pleasure, which are constantly fighting within you. You want things, but you cannot have them, so you are ready to kill; you strongly desire things, but you cannot get them, so you quarrel and fight" (James 3:16, 4:1-2; TEV).

As the Bible clearly states, greed and desire are at the root of this behavior, but sometimes the greed is not just for material things. The greed may be for love from the parents, which the adult child may feel she's been cheated of earlier in her life. What else can explain why children, after the parent's death, fight each other for things that have little monetary value? The value is in what the thing symbolizes, the parent's love.

If your parents' family house is in order, with all of its relationships healthy, then taking care of the financial house becomes relatively easy. There is no jealousy, envy, or greed to contend with. What a blessing for the heirs!

8

Where to Find the Help You Need

*God is our refuge and strength, a
very present help in trouble.*
Psalm 46:1, RSV

*God has appointed in the church
first apostles, second prophets, third
teachers, then workers of miracles,
then healers, helpers,
administrators, speakers in various
kinds of tongues.*
1 Corinthians 12:28, RSV; emphasis added

Caregivers may be crying to God for help, claiming the promises of Psalm 46:1 and other scriptures, and at the same time, fail to realize that His help usually comes to them from other people. It may come from the church, in which the helper is to play a prominent role, and if not from there, then from other community sources. God is sovereign—He can send help from any source He pleases.

But will caregivers accept it? Often they focus on asking God to give them the strength to do it themselves. It doesn't occur to them that "bear one another's burdens" means not only to give but to accept help when needed. Or, if they've expected their churches to help and have been disappointed when the churches haven't responded, they may not know where to turn.

Churches could perform a valuable service for caregivers by searching out available resources in their own communities and keeping this information on file. Often, a great deal of help is available for the elderly and their families, but it may not be easy to find. A caregiver can spend hours on the phone trying to find the right agency or person.

Social workers are professionals trained to know how to use community resources. Some large churches even have a social worker on staff to help people find their way through the maze of available services.

Social workers trained in gerontology may also be hired as private consultants (more about them later in this chapter), or you can seek out nurses with geriatric experience or experienced caregivers for advice. No matter what your problem may be, somebody else has probably been through it.

The help that may be most useful to you is the *assessment* of your elderly parent's needs. It may be difficult to know what she can do for herself and what she may need help in doing. Someone with experience in geriatrics will be able to judge how well she performs the Activities of Daily Living (ADLs), which are eating, bathing, dressing, toileting, transference (e.g., from bed to chair), and mobility, and the Instrumental Activities of Daily Living (IADLs), which are taking medications, meal preparation, managing money, making phone calls, doing laundry, light housework, shopping, errands, and transportation.

The professional doing the assessment could be a social worker from your county's social service department or a nurse trained in geriatrics from your county health department. Based on this assessment and your professional's recommendations, you can seek out the kind of assistance your parent needs.

A HELPING HAND FOR NORMAL AGING

A social worker or nurse experienced in working with the aging may also be able to suggest ways to help you or your parent adapt the home to compensate for some of the normal changes of aging that may make the ADLs and IADLs difficult for him.

Sensory losses in the aging body are a normal process. It's normal for aging eyes to see less sharply, distinguish colors with more difficulty, require more time to adjust to changes in light, need more light, and be sensitive to glare. In addition, nearly 30 percent of the aged have macular degeneration, a loss of central vision. Other common eye diseases are cataracts (clouding of the lenses), which is treated surgically, and glaucoma (increased pressure within the eyeball), which if untreated can cause blindness.

Some simple home adaptations can make a world of difference. Provide more light; the elderly need two to three times more wattage than people in their twenties. Use night-lights in bedrooms and bathrooms. Provide more contrast so that objects stand out against their backgrounds (for example, a white plate on a dark blue tablecloth or a dark switchplate on a light painted wall). Outline stair steps with contrasting color phosphorescent tape that glows in the dark.

Tactile tools help people with low vision continue to do

useful and enjoyable work. Or you can mark regular tools and household appliances by means of a raised line marker, which applies bright-orange raised dots from a squeeze tube. In addition to large-print books from the library, you can obtain large-print telephone touch dials and label objects with a large-print label maker. Needle threaders, yarn threaders, sewing machine magnifiers, and magnifiers with a neck strap are a few of the aids that will enable your parent to continue doing sewing and needlework. Many of these items are described in *The Gadget Book.* (See Appendix.)

Various low-vision aids use magnifying systems. If he's beyond using these, "Talking Books" on cassette tape are a free service of the Library of Congress, available through your public library. In addition, many bookstores now stock books on tape.

If you live near one of the Lighthouse for the Blind's more than 200 low-vision centers, or a local office of the American Foundation for the Blind, you can take your parent in to get help in finding ways to adapt to failing vision. Your local Lions Club may also have information.

Helping your parent adapt to hearing loss may be even more challenging. You may notice withdrawal and depression in your parent and never connect it with hearing loss. But often, when older people can no longer follow a conversation because of failing hearing, they begin to isolate themselves. Hearing loss can also lead to paranoia. Your parent doesn't hear well and begins to believe people must be talking about him. Or he distorts or misinterprets what's being said.

It doesn't bother most older people to wear eyeglasses, but for some reason, the need for a hearing aid is harder to accept. Your parent has probably heard from others that "hearing aids don't help anyway." But so much is at stake that nobody should deny themselves this help without a fair trial. It's possible now, for example, for your parent to get a hearing aid that magnifies only the sound frequencies he has trouble hearing. Some hearing aids are tiny enough to fit into the ear canal where they're all but invisible. Some have remote control switches. If you can persuade your parent to be tested by a qualified audiologist, the chances are good that he will be able to recommend a hearing aid that will help. Be sure to have your parent buy on a thirty-day trial basis so that the aid can be returned if it doesn't help. (Unfortunately, Medicare does not pay for hearing aids.)

Your parent doesn't have to turn up his radio or television to rock-concert volume in order to hear. A simple microphone and amplifier you can buy in any Radio Shack store will enable him to hear them tuned at normal levels. Telephone amplifiers and adapters are widely available. If you or your spouse are handy with tools, you can put together a home amplifying system with directions from a pamphlet called *Do-It-Yourself Listening and Signaling Devices for People with Hearing Impairment.* (See Appendix.) A number of devices on the market convert the sound of the telephone, doorbell, or smoke alarm to flashing lights. (See *The Gadget Book* listed in the Appendix.) A list of demonstration centers in the United States and Canada where people with hearing problems can see and test various assistive devices is available from Fellendorf Associates. (Address listed in the Appendix.)

Declines in the ability to taste and smell are subtle and may go unnoticed, but they can have serious health consequences. When food seems flavorless, the older person may lose his appetite and suffer weight loss and malnutrition. A decline in the sense of smell can be equally dangerous. Older people sometimes can't smell gas leaks, or decaying food in their refrigerators. Caregivers whose parents live independently should be alert for the smell of gas and check refrigerators and throw out food that shouldn't be eaten.

The skin grows thinner with age, and its sensitivity to touch declines. Oil glands become less active and blood circulation to the skin lessens. Thin skin is fragile. A touch that wouldn't mark a younger person's skin can leave cuts and bruises on an older person. It takes less pressure to make the skin break down, which increases the chance of bedsores in the bed-bound elderly. Dry skin can itch unbearably and needs less bathing and constant applications of lotion. Skin cancers also increase with age; any suspect spots should be seen by a dermatologist.

As we age, our bodies lose some of their ability to maintain normal body temperature. (Circulation problems are common in diabetics—see chapter 10 for more information.) The older person is more susceptible to extremes of heat and cold.

Hypothermia occurs when the body loses heat faster than it's replaced. At body temperatures below ninety-five degrees, vital organs may be damaged and death may result. This can happen, not just when the older person ventures outside in cold weather, but at home sitting in his own living room. The usual responses to cold of shivering and narrowing of blood vessels may be delayed or absent in an otherwise healthy older adult. The first symptoms of hypothermia may be slurred speech, sluggishness, or mental confusion. Some chronic diseases of the elderly, medications that are commonly prescribed to elderly people, and inadequate nutrition increase the risk of hypothermia.

Prevention is simple: the elderly must keep warm. Experts recommend a thermostat setting of a least seventy degrees. It's been my experience that many elderly people feel cold at a seventy-degree setting, although younger people in the same room are perfectly comfortable. The elderly can simply wear more clothing indoors. Fleece-lined warmup suits make good daywear and nightwear for the elderly during the winter.

Space heaters can be used to supplement central heating. Electric heaters are safer than oil or kerosene-burning heaters, which can pollute indoor air and can be a fire hazard. All heaters should have a safety device that cuts the heater off when it's tipped over. Electric blankets help at night, but only if the elder is mentally alert enough to regulate it. (Electric blankets and electric heating pads can burn—and since the older person's skin is not as sensitive, he may not feel it until it's too late.)

If your parent's home is inadequately heated or insulated, he may be eligible for help from the federally-funded Low Income Home Energy Assistance Program or the Low Income Weatherization Program, both administered through local governments.

If hypothermia does occur in the elderly, treat it as a medical emergency. The same is true of heat stroke and heat exhaustion. The majority of people who die during an extreme heat wave are elderly. Prevention consists of staying inside during the heat of the day, dressing in cool, loose-fitting clothing, drinking more fluids, and keeping fans and air conditioning working.

As we age, we lose muscle mass, resulting in declining physical strength and problems with mobility. Many elderly people also suffer from osteoarthritis, which results in stiff and sore muscles and joints. Other chronic diseases can also leave your parent weakened and less mobile.

A great deal of research points to the benefits of exercise at every age (including very advanced age) in preventing muscle weakness and staying mobile. The very worse thing your parents can do is sit or lie in bed too much, but unfortunately, this may be the very thing the elderly want to do. They believe they've earned the right to rest, and they may think you're mean and unfeeling to want them to move more.

However, seeing is believing. If you can persuade them to enroll in an exercise program suited to their capabilities, and they begin to feel better, they may believe you. Both the Arthritis Foundation and the Easter Seal Society have exercise programs for the disabled in many locations. Their local chapters can help your parent in coping with mobility problems. (See chapter 10 for more information.)

You may be amazed at the number of adaptive devices on the market to make living easier for persons with physical handicaps. Utensils and household tools with easy-grip handles for arthritic hands, tools that can be used one-handed, devices to make dressing easier such as elastic shoelaces and Velcro-closed shoes and clothing, non-skid matting to anchor dishes on the table, and a foot mop that lets you dust the floor with your feet are some of the handy gadgets that can help your parent maintain his independence as long as possible.

However, you won't find many of these devices at your local store. Most are available only through mail-order sources. If you have specific questions, the National Rehabilitation Information Center's (NRIC) computerized databank, ABLEDATA is just a phone call away. (See the Appendix.) ABLEDATA can provide the names of specific devices to help your parent and tell you where to buy them. Most of NRIC's services are free.

If and when your parent needs a cane, walker, or wheelchair, Medicare will usually pay for them if a doctor prescribes them. Other aids you might not think of include raised toilet seats and commode bars, catapult seats and chairs, and chair leg extenders to raise the height of chairs, making them easier for elderly people to get out of. Some of these are available through local medical and home health supply stores. Many people are not aware that the Easter Seal Society lends a great deal of this type of equipment and helps low-income families toward their purchase.

WHAT IF YOUR PARENT DOESN'T WANT HELP?

Your parent's pride may make it difficult for her to accept help from you even when it will keep her living independently. Sometimes an outside person, such as a social worker or nurse, may succeed where you fail. Or your parent may not want help from anybody outside the family. Her generation got through the Great Depression, a world war, and numerous other crises without help from any "outsiders." She may tell you that she'll never accept charity!

Explain, as often as necessary, why you can't do everything yourself. Continue to remind her of your joint goal: to keep her in her own home (or if she's living with you, in your home) as long as possible. Bringing in help is the only way to achieve this goal.

If the help is from a social service agency, point out that this is not charity. You and she have paid taxes for this service; you are merely getting back a small part of what you've already paid into the system. If the help is from volunteers, point out that she's helped people all her life; now it's her turn to be on the receiving end. Tell her refusing help is the same as turning her back on God, who works through people. If she's too proud to accept help from God, then she's too proud!

WHAT COMMUNITY SERVICES ARE AVAILABLE?

Most urban and suburban areas make the following services available to your parent, whether she's living independently or with you:

▶Nutrition sites—a center, usually a school, where one hot meal per day is served to seniors. The social value of eating with a group is almost as important as the meal.

▶Home-delivered meals—a hot meal ("Meals on Wheels") once a day delivered by volunteers.

▶Transportation—to doctors' appointments, senior centers, etc. Some senior transportation vans are equipped with wheelchair lifts.

▶Housing—subsidized housing for low-income seniors. (However, in some localities, these have long waiting lists.)

▶Financial assistance for the low-income elderly in paying for heating fuel and home insulation.

▶Senior centers—providing recreation, crafts, classes, and opportunities for socializing. Some provide services, such as help with income taxes and health insurance forms, on site.

▶Safety checks—a telephone service in which a volunteer contacts the senior by telephone daily. Many hospitals offer electronic communications (often called "Lifelines"). The senior wears a device that alerts the hospital switchboard, when a button is pressed, that she needs help.

▶Health services—usually includes public health nurses and clinics. This is not always just for the low-income elderly. In some localities, doctors and dentists make house calls.

▶Home health care—Medicare pays for only a limited amount of nursing and personal service delivered to the home. Some long-term care insurance policies cover this. It is expensive if hired through private agencies.

Other services that may not be as widely available include:

▶Legal assistance.

▶Help with filling out Social Security, income tax, and Medicare forms; help in applying for Medicaid and Supplemental Security Income (SSI) and in choosing health insurance. If these services are not available through volunteers in your community, private businesses provide them for a fee.

▶Housekeeping services for the low-income disabled and/or elderly.

▶Referral lists—lists of workers available for house-keeping, of board-and-care homes, and of convalescent hospitals.

▶Case management—counseling for the elderly and their families; help with finding needed services.

▶Adult day-care services—a place where the impaired and frail elderly can be cared for and can socialize, providing respite for their caregivers.

▶Home delivery services—groceries, medicines, dry cleaning, etc.

Often you can find out about these services in your community with one phone call. The Older Americans Act of

1975 established 662 Area Agencies on Aging (AAA; also called Councils on Aging in some localities) to dispense information to the elderly and their families. If you visit in person, you should find helpful informational leaflets and brochures from service providers.

If your first phone call doesn't give you what you need, don't give up. You may have reached a volunteer who's not particularly knowledgeable. Keep calling; ask to speak to the director; persist until you get answers to your questions.

You should be able to find the number for your local AAA in the yellow pages of your phone book under "seniors" or "elderly" or in the white pages under the government listings. If that doesn't work, call your local library, and if they can't help, call the local office of your congressional representative.

One referral may lead to another—for example, your AAA may refer you to the local housing authority, which may refer you to social services, etc. Be patient; it may take time to work your way through the system.

"AGING IN PLACE"

This lovely slogan describes what happens when elderly people are able to stay in their homes, among familiar surroundings. Many communities provide services because it's much healthier for seniors, and much less expensive for taxpayers, to help them to stay in their own homes than to place them in nursing homes.

However, your parents may have problems remaining in their homes. They may not be able to afford the taxes. They may no longer be able to make the necessary repairs themselves, and they may not have the money to hire someone to do this. Rising prices may make it difficult for them to pay for heating fuel. How can they find the money to stay?

A relatively new plan called Home Equity Conversion (also called the Reverse Annuity Mortgage in some parts of the country) will enable them to draw on the equity in their homes for income. While the reverse mortgage has been available in some localities for years, a law that went into effect in 1989 authorizes the U.S. Department of Housing and Urban Development (HUD) to implement a Home Equity Conversion Insurance Demonstration Program, which should greatly expand the number of available loans.

How does the plan work? Home Equity Conversion Loans (HECs) enable your parents to continue living in their homes for the duration of their lifetimes. The plan pays the home-owner a fixed monthly payment for a certain number of years or the homeowner's lifetime (depending on the plan). At the end of that time, the loan plus interest becomes due. If the estate cannot pay it, the mortgage holder claims the property. Your parent, in effect, gives up his home in return for the right to live in it for his lifetime and to have enough income to pay the taxes and make needed repairs. Unlike home equity loans, no payments are due on the loan during his lifetime.

HECs are available from private banks and financial institutions and some state and local agencies. There is some financial risk, and the American Association of Retired Persons (AARP), which has been monitoring these plans, advises caution in selecting them. (A free AARP booklet on HECs, "Home-Made Money," is listed in the Appendix.)

HOME SHARING BY ELDERS

The parent who lives in a spacious home can sometimes afford to stay there by sharing it with others. She can rent out rooms or share the costs as well as the space with a housemate. If she chooses the former, she'll still have all the responsibilities of a landlady. Is she capable of handling them? If she opts for the latter, then compatibility becomes an issue. Some people have been able to exchange room and board with a younger person in exchange for services such as housekeeping or yard work.

Obviously, you or your parent should check references carefully and go slowly before you let anybody move into her house. There is always the possibility of abuse when a frail elder lives with a younger, stronger person. A few communities around the country have referral services to match up people needing housing with people who have housing to offer. (Check with your local AAA or the Shared Housing Resource Center in Philadelphia listed in the Appendix, which has more than 400 shared housing program affiliates nationwide.)

HELP WITH HEALTH CARE COSTS

Most Americans over sixty-five depend on Medicare, the U.S. government's health insurance program, for help in paying the increased medical costs that come with aging. However, in recent years, Medicare costs to the government have sky-rocketed, while the elderly continue to pay more and more.

Many of your parent's most pressing health care needs are not covered by Medicare. Medicare does not pay for routine physicals, immunizations, eyeglasses, dentures, hearing aids, and long-term care (home health care and nursing homes). In addition, your parent must pay certain deductibles and coinsurance charges before Medicare will pay his medical costs. If his physician does not accept what Medicare pays ("Medicare assignment"), he is responsible for paying the difference between the Medicare reimbursement and the doctor's actual bill.

Congress attempted to remedy some of the problems with Medicare by passing the Medicare Catastrophic Coverage Act of 1988. While this increases some coverages, it also requires Medicare recipients above 85 percent of the federal poverty line to pay additional premiums every month.

What help can your parent currently expect from Medicare? Under the new act, Medicare Part A still pays for all covered hospital costs for up to sixty days with a $540 deductible, and up to 150 days in a skilled nursing facility with a coinsurance payment for the first eight days. Hospice and some home health care are also covered. Custodial care (board-and-care and nursing homes) is not.

Medicare Part B covers physicians, outpatient treatment, and ambulance services. Beginning in 1991, part of the cost of drugs will be covered. Beginning in 1989, spouses of nursing home patients were given some relief. Instead of requiring that a couple's total assets be used for nursing home care, the law now allows the noninstitutionalized spouse to keep $786 per month and either $12,000 or half the couple's assets, whichever is greater. Other additional benefits will be phased in over a four-year period; for example, some payment for respite care begins in 1990.

Unlike Medicare, Medicaid is a welfare program administered by each state for persons below a certain income level. If your parents' medical expenses reduce their assets enough, they will qualify to receive Medicaid. If they are disabled, they may also qualify for Supplemental Security Income (SSI) available through Social Security. For assistance in helping your parents apply, call your city or county social services department.

Since 1985, the government has allowed Medicare benefits to pay for costs of a health maintenance organization (HMO), and many retirees choose this option. An HMO is a prepaid plan. Members pay a flat monthly or yearly fee, which covers all treatment received. (Some also require small co-payments per treatment.) HMOs are a low-cost alternative, but they do have disadvantages. Patients must be treated by the HMO doctors, or specialists to whom they're referred by the HMO doctor. Any other treatment will be paid out of the patient's own pocket.

HMOs also have their problems. Their numbers have increased rapidly in the eighties. Some have been unable to meet the competition, others have been badly managed and are experiencing financial difficulties and bankruptcy, leaving their members without medical services. Complaints about troubled HMOs include long waits for doctor's appointments and poor services from rushed, overworked physicians, resulting in misdiagnosis and inadequate care. If your parents are considering joining an HMO, encourage them to choose carefully. Is the HMO they're considering financially sound? Are its members satisfied with the services they're receiving? (In order to find out, ask people who are members.)

Buying Medical Insurance

Most older Americans who can afford it buy supplementary insurance to cover some of the costs not covered by Medicare. (These are called "Medigap" policies.) The trend in private health insurance is less coverage for higher costs as insurance companies pass along increased medical costs to the consumer. For your parents to get their money's worth, they need to exercise extreme caution. If they need help, you should compare policies and ask a lot of questions. Don't be confused by high pressure salespeople. There is no such thing as a policy that covers all costs not covered by Medicare. And there is no need to buy more than one "Medigap" policy. (Insurance counseling may be available at your local agency on aging.)

Is the purchase of long-term care (nursing home) insurance a good idea for your parents? Perhaps. This is a new and relatively untried insurance product; but nursing home costs are so frightening (averaging $22,000 per year in 1988) that sales of long-term care insurance policies have gone from almost nothing in 1984 to over half a million policies in 1988, and the trend continues upward.

Long-term care insurance is expensive. Currently, premiums range from $400 to $1200 per year and will certainly rise in the future along with nursing home costs. The older you are at the time you enroll, the more you will pay. Help your parents know what they're buying. Many policies have so many exclusions that your parents may never collect. For example, many early policies did not pay unless the insured entered a nursing home after a three-day or longer stay at an acute care hospital. Alzheimer's patients may not need to be hospitalized before entering a nursing home, so their nursing home policy won't pay.

Most policies pay nursing home costs for one year, some for two. Since the average nursing home stay is fifteen months, this will cover most people. But if your parent is unlucky enough to be among the four-to-five percent of patients who stay longer, his coverage will run out.

The benefits of long-term care insurance have to be weighed against the risks. According to Galen Irens, director of a state-funded Health Insurance Care and Advocacy Program (HICAP) in California, the major reason for buying such a policy is to protect an estate. If your parent doesn't have much money, it will run out quickly and he'll soon be on Medicaid anyway. On the other hand, if the estate is a large one, income from investments may be sufficient to pay nursing home fees. You need to know the amount of your parent's estate (if there is one), and then you need to obtain sound financial advice on protecting it. (See chapter 7.)

WHEN A PARENT LIVES AT A DISTANCE

The frail, elderly parent who lives at a distance presents a caregiving dilemma. She needs help, yet you're too far away to provide it. Your parent has some social support from family and friends where she is, but it's not possible for them to take over her care. If you move her closer to you or into your home, will she be socially isolated and lonely? A long-distance move is stressful at any age, and especially so for the elderly who have enough other stresses already. What really is best?

If enough services for seniors are available in her community, and if there is enough money to hire additional care, it may be possible to keep her in her home even though you live at a distance. Through one of the networks for senior care listed in the Appendix, you may be able to find a private care-manager in her locality who will act on your behalf.

What does a care-manager do? One day, I accompanied Mary Thorman, who has a Master's degree in social work and is the owner of TLC for Seniors in St. Petersburg, Florida, on her daily rounds. Mary is one of a growing number of social workers trained in gerontology who provide this service for families.

Our first visit was to Sarah Smith, eighty-six, an unmarried former schoolteacher who had retired to Florida over twenty-five years ago. Emma Anderson, a housekeeper-companion that Mary had hired, greeted us at the door of Sarah's home. Emma, a slim, energetic lady with an enormous smile, lives with Sarah four-and-a-half days per week. She takes care of all of Sarah's needs, bathing her, shampooing and setting her hair, helping her dress, and driving her to the doctor and to the mall in Sarah's car. She keeps the house spotless and, under Mary's supervision, hires other workers to take care of the lawn and do necessary maintenance and repair work on the house.

Mary's visit was eagerly anticipated. Emma proudly displayed her folder with a place for incoming bills and a brown manila petty cash envelope. Sarah's income is deposited directly into her bank account. Mary pays Sarah's bills and gives her spending money, which Emma keeps track of. It's important for Sarah to feel she has some control of her own money, yet before Mary started the present system, Sarah had withdrawn sums of cash from her account and hidden the bills between pages of newspapers, which were subsequently thrown out.

Mary spent about an hour with Sarah and Emma, discussing Sarah's health and the bills that needed to be paid and directing Emma to call plumbers and get bids for needed repairs. They also discussed Sarah's need for a new television set and what kind to get.

TLC for Seniors charges $37.50 per hour for services to its elderly clients. (Costs nationwide vary from approximately $25 to $50 per hour.) Included in the billing is the time spent on home visits, writing checks and balancing bank accounts, taking clients to the doctor, visiting them when hospitalized, and telephoning on the client's behalf. Mary acts as her clients' advocate with "the system," just as a caregiving member of the family would. But, as a professional social worker, she has the advantage of knowing the system much better than the average caregiver would.

TLC was hired by Sarah's only remaining relative, a nephew living "up North." Sarah is the last of five children and inherited most of the family's money, so she can well afford Mary's services. TLC pays, with Sarah's funds, $250 per week to Emma and $90 for relief care on weekends.

I was not allowed to go into the home on Mary's second visit. The woman was becoming paranoid and believed TLC for Seniors was possessed by evil spirits. Undoubtedly, Mary told me, physical problems were behind this paranoia, but her client, a Christian Scientist, would not allow Mary to take her to a doctor. I waited in the car.

Our third visit was to Anna Boyd, an eighty-five-year-old single lady also living alone in her own home. In striking contrast to Sarah's, this house was cluttered and worn, with paint peeling off the walls. Anna has no money of her own; a well-to-do nephew pays for TLC's services.

Although Mary has recommended live-in help, Anna has refused. We found her sitting at her dining room table, her walker nearby. She'd recently had a stroke that caused her to fall, and she lay on the floor all night before help arrived. She'd badly bruised her back and neck and suffered a wound in her leg that still had not healed. Although her speech seemed slurred, her mind was alert.

Finally, Anna has agreed to wear the Lifeline signaling device for emergencies that Mary had been urging on her. Mary has to raise her voice considerably when she speaks to her. Anna is growing deaf but won't be tested for a hearing aid and has failing eyesight but won't let Mary take her to an eye doctor. If Mary's efforts to persuade her clients don't work, there's nothing she can do. TLC is no different in that respect from any family caregiver.

Mary discussed the leg with Anna. If there is no improvement by next week, she said, she will make a doctor's appointment for her. They discussed a tax bill for the house, and Mary asked if Anna's garage apartment tenant had paid his rent in cash. (His previous checks had bounced.) They also discussed Anna's ne'er-do-well nephew who visits from time to time, borrowing money and running up long-distance phone bills.

"Don't let him make any phone calls," Mary warned. (But, I wondered, if her nephew wanted to call from her phone, how would this frail, handicapped little lady stop him?)

Until you have witnessed visits such as these, it's impossible to fully appreciate the vulnerability and helplessness of the frail elderly. What of those who can't afford to hire private care management such as TLC for Seniors?

Some localities do provide this service for the low-income, frail elderly. St. Petersburg provides state-funded care management through its Community Care for the Elderly. However, there is a long waiting list to receive this service.

IF YOU CAN AFFORD TO PAY FOR SERVICES

When you act as your parent's care-manager, you have the responsibility of hiring and supervising paid workers. I once thought this was an "easy" alternative to nursing home care, but I soon learned differently. It's almost a full-time career in itself.

Where do you begin looking for paid workers? If your local agency on aging provides a list of available people, you could start with that. I started by placing a help-wanted notice on the bulletin board in the laundry room of my parents' apartment complex. When someone living in the complex applied for the job, the apartment manager vouched for her honesty and reliability.

A help-wanted notice on your local senior center's bulletin board is another possibility. You could advertise in a senior center's newsletter, if there is one, in church newsletters in your community, or in the local newspaper. You could also ask the teacher of a home health aide course in your community for recommendations of recent graduates.

Another alternative is a home health care agency. You will pay more, but reputable agencies screen workers to eliminate possible thieves, alcoholics, and drug addicts. Some agencies also train their own workers or require them to have certification. Agencies also provide backup workers in case your helper is not able to come. This could be crucial if you must go to your own job.

The agencies' charges cover the necessary paperwork and employers' contributions to Social Security taxes, federal and state tax withholding, and worker's compensation insurance, all of which are required by law.

Caregivers who hire workers directly sometimes get around this by hiring them as "independent contractors" rather than as employees. (However, if the Internal Revenue Service [IRS] questions this, the burden of proof will be on you.) I know of caregivers who have been sued by disgruntled former employees for back wages and reported to state wage-and-hour boards and other regulatory bodies. Protect yourself by getting up-to-date information on tax laws and wage-and-hour laws from the IRS, state tax board, and state regulatory agencies. Keep accurate records of hours worked and amounts paid and file receipts or cancelled checks.

In hiring workers, you will need to be very clear about the duties; training required, if any; the hours; and the wages you are willing to pay.

What will the costs be? Agencies currently charge from $8 to $10 per hour for housekeeper-companions (no personal care duties); from $12 to $14 per hour for home health aides; and from $23 to $25 for LPNs. Hourly charges for night duty are higher. Agency charges for live-in help range from $90 to $124 per twenty-four-hour day. Deduct 25 to 30 percent from these costs if you hire workers directly instead of through an agency. Costs will be lower in small towns and rural areas. Some of these costs may be tax deductible from either your parents' income taxes or yours; see your tax advisor for current rules.

Have a list of requirements and questions ready to ask so that you can screen applicants by phone. Interview in person only those who seem most promising.

I'd recommend that you interview workers twice, once by yourself and again in the presence of your parent, observing how the prospective employee relates to her. In my opinion, warmth and caring are more important than technical proficiency. Perhaps the most important question you can ask is "What kind of a relationship did you have with your grandparents?" Almost without exception, those who work best with the elderly are people who had a close, loving relationship in childhood with one or more grandparents.

Monitoring Care

You may have heard that home health care is the wave of the future, that it's going to keep the elderly out of nursing homes, and other such optimistic statements. What nobody tells you is that, without careful supervision and monitoring, home health care doesn't work. The elderly person can't oversee it himself; if he were well enough to hire and supervise workers, he might not need them. These responsibilities are yours.

Workers who show up late or don't show up at all, workers who watch television all day and ignore your parent, workers who call in sick when you have no replacement, even workers who are abusive—these are some of the potential hazards of hiring home health care.

If the worker is to be at your parent's home, supervision and monitoring become extremely difficult. Connie, a Christian caregiver who has hired help for her geographically distant parents for years, has had to rely on her parents' neighbors to alert her when things go wrong. And they have. One live-in worker moved her boyfriend into the house. Another charged food for her large family to Connie's parents. One aide sent by an agency turned out to be deaf and did not hear calls for help.

Lest you become too frightened by these stories to hire help, let me hasten to say that some of the kindest, most devoted, and most loving and caring women I've ever met were the selfless people I was able to hire to help me care for my mother. They were jewels.

HELP ON THE HORIZON

Clearly, the cost of hiring significant amounts of home help is too high for the majority of families. Few qualify for the limited amount of aid available to low-income elderly. Some attempts to come up with a solution for those in the middle are on the horizon.

The National Long-Term Care Channeling Demonstration is an experiment being carried out by ten agencies across the country selected by the U.S. Department of Health and Welfare. The agencies are both public, such as Area Agencies on Aging, and private, such as the Miami Jewish Home and Hospital for the Aged in Miami, Florida. They use professional care-managers who draw on a combination of community resources.

The consensus of the project directors so far is that they had underestimated the amount of time needed to assure the *quality* of in-home care. In other words, they ran into exactly the same sort of problems experienced by family caregivers.

In 1985, the U.S. Health Care Finance Administration began four demonstration Social Health Maintenance Organization (SHMO) projects in Oregon, California, Minnesota, and New York. Like Health Maintenance Organizations (HMOs) the SHMO is a prepaid plan with the addition of social services, which are brought into the home. Enrollees pay from $25 to $49 per person per month for personal care, home nursing and therapy, housekeeping, adult day care, medical transportation, etc., as needed. A case-manager decides who will receive services, and which ones will be provided. There is a financial cap on services ranging from $450 to $1000 per person per month.

Similar projects have also been funded by private foundations. The Robert Wood Johnson Foundation has twenty-four projects around the country designed to keep the elderly in their homes. An example is the "Life Care at Home" program run by FRC Management Corporation, a nonprofit corporation set up by Folkways Retirement Community of the Society of Friends (Quakers) in Philadelphia in partnership with a Philadelphia hospital. In this plan, enrollees pay an entry fee of up to $5000 (based on age at entry) and monthly fees. Members are also charged copayments for medical visits, medicine, eye care, etc. Care-managers decide who needs additional in-home services and what services will be provided.

This is really a new and experimental type of insurance plan, and only time will tell if it will work. Its success will depend on selling it to enough people to get it started and keeping operating costs below the income from premiums. Since future costs are unpredictable, the financial projections may not work out.

WHAT CAN CHURCHES DO TO HELP YOU?

Help from churches for families of the elderly is currently like a "cloud no bigger than a man's hand."

When one caregiver and her husband moved her ninety-eight-year-old mother into their home, their church came through with a list of people available to give respite care whenever they needed to get away. But my experience suggests that this is the exception rather than the rule. Most caregivers I've spoken to say, "I don't get any support from my church."

Churches that are effective in ministry to the elderly and their families often use the offices of deacon and deaconess as a means of channeling care. Churches with strong adult Sunday schools often find that the Sunday school class is a natural caring unit. Both could be strengthened by training, but leadership to do this must come from the pastor.

One barrier to "equipping the saints" for work with the elderly is the lack of training in gerontology in our nation's seminaries. However, this need not stop anyone from learning. The best practical teachers are not always the academics and the professionals but lay people with valuable on-the-job training. One service that you, as a caregiver, can do for your church leaders is to share your suffering with them. By doing so, you will be helping to train them for future service.

If your church leaders express interest, you could also do a great service to others by suggesting training materials. At this writing, The Christian Action Council is developing "Project Mercy: A Ministry to the Elderly and Terminally Ill," a videotape series to train lay Christians. Carol Spargo Pierskalla, Ph.D., director of Aging Today and Tomorrow for the American Baptist Churches in the U.S.A., and Jane Dewey Heald, M.S., former executive director of the National Support Center for Families of the Aging, have developed "Help for Families of the Aging," a training course designed to help caregivers spiritually and emotionally. Many denominations have also developed training materials on working with the elderly and their families. (See the Appendix.)

Information about church programs that could serve as models is available from the National Interfaith Coalition on Aging. The newly formed Forum for Religion and Aging of the American Society on Aging acts as a clearinghouse for programs on aging and puts on workshops and training sessions. (Addresses for this resource and others are listed in the Appendix.) You could also try to interest your church leaders in starting a support group for caregivers.

In recent years, many churches have provided space for adult day care of various types. Often these are run by outside community agencies with or without the help of volunteers from the congregation. In addition to providing respite for caregivers, they give isolated seniors much-needed social contacts and stimulation. For example, in an Alzheimer's Respite Center at St. Clement's Episcopal Church in Berkeley, California, Alzheimer's patients who might have been sitting and staring into space at home become more animated and lively. They respond well to music, singing, dancing, or clapping their hands, and they enjoy simple games.

Unfortunately, church members may hesitate to volunteer at such centers because they're "depressing." But when I visited the Berkeley center, I found it anything but. Roberta, the director, hugs and kisses every patient who comes in.

There are enough volunteers for an almost one-on-one inter-action with the patients. I watched a white-haired older couple who had been married for sixty-two years. He (the caregiver) was a dapper gentleman. His wife (the Alzheimer's patient) was beautifully coiffed and dressed in a red wool suit. They held hands and beamed at each other. He led her out to dance—she was still, in his adoring eyes, the belle of the ball. There was so much love in that room, I forgot to be sad. People need to learn this.

Churches can accomplish a great deal for the elderly and their families by pooling their resources. In 1984, the Robert Wood Johnson Foundation funded twenty-five interfaith vol-unteer projects around the country. About one hundred others are also in operation. Together they make up the National Federation of Interfaith Volunteer Caregivers, Inc. (IVC).

These projects draw their volunteers from a number of churches in a community—at least twelve to fourteen congre-gations are needed to make the plan work. Each project has a paid director and a coordinator of volunteers within each congregation. The project director is responsible for publiciz-ing the service and reaching into the community to find older people needing assistance. Volunteers from the various con-gregations are then matched to those needing help. Among the services offered are transportation, visitation, advocacy/referral, home care, shopping, chores, respite care, etc. Most volunteers receive some training, and in the majority of cases, a close personal "family" type of relationship develops be-tween those giving and those receiving assistance. (For more information, contact the Robert Wood Johnson Foundation or the IVC Federation, listed in the Appendix.)

If you have sought help in your church and community without finding it, perhaps God is calling you, as a caregiver, to help your church find new ways it can serve the elderly.

9

Where Can Your Parent Live?

Do not cast me off in the time of old age; forsake me not when my strength is spent.
Psalm 71:9, RSV

Survey after survey has shown that the overwhelming majority of older Americans wish to remain in their own homes. Yet for many (perhaps most) elderly people, illness or frailty may make that impossible. Perhaps you have done your best as a caregiver to help your parent stay in her own home but find that it is no longer working.

If and when that time comes, your parent may feel abandoned—cast off and forsaken. But this isn't true. You can still help her to find alternatives. A nursing home is not the only choice left. And even if it is, reassure her that you and the rest of the family will not be abandoning her.

Ideally, your parent should make the decision to change her living arrangements herself, but that isn't always an option. In general, the more money available, the more choices she will have. But the choices must be made at the right time. Most housing for the elderly requires that the people moving in be in good enough health to care for themselves. If your parents wait until one or both of them are disabled, they will not be able to get in. When and if a crisis occurs that makes a move necessary, you will have to act, perhaps without being able to consult them or to make as good a choice as you might have with their cooperation.

GROUP HOME ARRANGEMENTS

In addition to match-up programs, The National Shared Housing Resource Center (NSHRC) has information on agencies around the country that sponsor group shared residences. The sponsoring agency owns and operates a house that is shared by unrelated individuals (usually from four to eight people). An example is St. Peter's House in Philadelphia, an intergenerational, interracial household of eight residents living in a three-story Victorian house that was formerly the rectory of St. Peter's Episcopal Church. It's managed by the NSHRC in conjunction with Episcopal Community Services and Rouse Urban Housing, Inc.

Group homes vary a great deal in their makeup and governance. Some are managed by the residents themselves, while others receive services that the sponsoring agency contracts for, such as housekeeping, yard maintenance, meals, laundry, etc. How well these arrangements work depends not only on the flexibility and compatibility of the residents but on how well they are supervised by the sponsoring agency.

CONTINUING CARE RETIREMENT COMMUNITIES

For those who can afford it, live-in retirement communities offer independent living for the able senior but have services in place that can be utilized by residents who become incapacitated while in residence. Some have nursing homes on the same grounds and are often referred to as life care communities. Continuing Care Retirement Communities (CCRCs) is a more general term.

Originally, most of these care communities were sponsored by church denominations, which set up nonprofit corporations to build and manage the facilities, usually with minimal church involvement and supervision. But recently, private enterprise has seen an opportunity to provide this type of housing profitably to an aging population. Marriott and Hyatt, two hotel chains, began constructing CCRCs in the eighties, but there are also many smaller companies entering this market.

The advantages of the CCRCs, for those who can afford them, are the availability of services already on the premises and the social stimulation provided by other residents and planned activities. This is no small contribution to your parent's health. The world of an elderly person living alone or isolated in your home often shrinks to four walls and a television set. Loneliness and isolation cause depression, depression worsens physical problems, and a vicious cycle is set up. CCRCs may be the answer for those who can adjust to them, and many do—very happily.

"Marvel Mansions" and Zion Home: Commercial CCRCs

An example of the new, privately built CCRC is a retirement center in my area I'll call "Marvel Mansions." It consists of a group of three-story apartment buildings and a one-story wing for the dining room, common living areas, and administrative offices. The grounds are attractively landscaped. A standard one-bedroom, 480-square-foot apartment consists of a living-dining area with kitchenette, a bedroom with queen-size bed, two closets, a bath, and either a patio or balcony.

Included in the monthly fees (rent), which started at $1095 in 1988, are utilities, three meals per day in the central dining room, housekeeping and laundry, a van for transportation to nearby shopping centers, churches, and medical appointments, and a schedule of planned social and recreational activities. A general store/gift shop, beauty parlor, and barbershop are on the premises.

In addition, there is a separate building for seniors needing assistance with daily living. It provides all services plus personal care and assistance with medications provided by the home health division of a local hospital. The home health care fees are additional.

Unlike many life care facilities, Marvel Mansions charges no entrance fees and has no leases with residents, who are free to move at any time. Like any private landlord, it can, and undoubtedly will, raise the rents and fees to cover increased future costs. If residents become unable to pay, they must move. If they require skilled nursing care, they will also have to move. There is no nursing home and there are no plans to build one. Obviously, without a nursing home, Marvel Mansions offers no guarantee of lifelong care.

Another type of congregate living arrangement has been provided by Zion Home, a care home affiliated with a major Protestant denomination for over fifty years. Zion Home offers four levels of care. The first is an independent living unit: studio, one-, and two-bedroom apartments with complete kitchens and a basement parking garage for residents, many of whom are still driving their cars. At this level, taking meals in the dining room is optional. Included in the fees are all utilities, heavy cleaning (outside windows, carpets, and drapes), and bus transportation to shopping centers and church services. Nurses and physicians are on call. Planned activities are available if desired.

On the second level are personal care units—private rooms located in the large main building, plus some cottages. Residents of these units eat in the central dining room and receive housekeeping and laundry services, as well as take part in planned activities. Registered nurses are on duty around the clock.

Those who need more help with the activities of daily living can move to the next level, assisted-living. Here residents are provided with meal service in the rooms, assistance with medications, bathing, dressing, etc., and nursing supervision as needed. However, assisted-living residents do not receive around-the-clock skilled nursing care.

The fourth and final level is a skilled nursing facility. Admission to this nursing home is from within Zion Home only; no "outsiders" are accepted. Nursing home residents pay the full, private nursing home fees of over $20,000 per year. When their assets are exhausted, they have to go on Medicaid.

Residents of Zion Home are admitted at the independent living or personal care levels, by approval of an application that requests financial information and a medical examination by a physician. Entrance fees range from $20,000 to $50,000 for an independent living apartment and from $3,000 to $12,000 for a personal care unit, plus monthly fees starting at $375. In addition, residents are required to lend Zion Home from $20,000 to $30,000. Entrance fees are not returned; loans, plus interest, are returned to the resident's estate after his or her death.

Most residents finance their entrance with the proceeds of homes that have appreciated enormously in value. This usually represents all or almost all of their assets. A few who are not able to pay the full fee are subsidized. Those who move in and later become unable to pay the full fees are not asked to move. Grants from foundations and donations from church members and congregations help to pay these costs.

Dangers of Life Care Arrangements

CCRCs are not without their risks. People who buy into them are not buying any equity in the community. They're receiving an "occupancy license" that entitles them to reside there. This "occupancy license" will become worthless if, at some future time, CCRC runs into financial difficulties.

That's exactly what happened in 1977 when Pacific Homes, a chain of life care communities sponsored by the United Methodist Church, filed for bankruptcy in California. During the late seventies, many life care communities ran into financial trouble. Better medical care was extending life for more people, and they were outliving their assets. At the same time, double-digit inflation was sending day-to-day living expenses and medical expenses out of control.

Also, at that time, there was no state or federal regulation of these institutions. (Regulation is still minimal.) Fraud ran rampant; in Florida, a life care retirement village sponsored by the Michigan Baptist Foundation was shut down by the State of Florida Division of Securities, and three Foundation officers were indicted for fraud and selling unregistered securities. Some residents of the village had bought bonds to build the community, planning to rely on interest from the bonds to pay their monthly fees. They lost everything. Contrary to the investors' belief, the Foundation was not financially guaranteed, nor was it overseen, by the Baptist church.

The National Consumer League, in its publication "A Consumer Guide to Life Care Communities," warns of the potential for fraud and mismanagement. Some of the fraudulent claims made by these communities have included implying that they had church affiliations, claiming that a religious organization had financial responsibility over them, misrepresenting the mortgage lender's responsibility, and misrepresenting the community's financial assets.

Since AARP has estimated that one such community in ten goes bankrupt or gets into financial difficulties, you and your parents should approach life care plans with caution, especially those which require large sums of money "up front."

Those who have comparison-shopped for CCRCs tell me that the range of choices is huge and bewildering. No two plans seem to be alike, which makes comparison difficult. In general, these are the most important questions to ask:

1) How long has this CCRC been in existence? Is it full and does it stay full, with a waiting list? You're looking for management with a good track record, one able to keep the facility occupied, since under-occupancy is one of the main reasons for financial problems.

2) Is there a nursing home or home health care on the premises? Does it carry an additional charge, and if so, how much?

3) What are the health requirements for entrance? Do they take the physically or mentally impaired? Under what health circumstances can you be forced to give up your apartment or room?

4) Can you enter for a trial period (thirty to ninety days) and receive a refund if you decide not to stay?

5) How will future monthly increases be handled? A contract without allowance for future increases is financially unsound, but there should be some limit, perhaps tied to consumer price index increases, or an upper limit of five percent.

6) If you become unable to pay the charges, will you be forced to move? (Nonprofit communities must guarantee the resident a lifetime apartment or lose nonprofit status.)

7) Will they allow your accountant to check the books?

You will also want a lawyer and an accountant familiar with life care arrangements to check the contract and the actuarial projections, annual report, and other documents.

CCRCs are not for everyone, but for those who can afford them they offer companionship, social stimulation, and peace of mind. Many elderly people have entered too depressed to get out of bed and have been coaxed back to life. Some (but not all) of the church-affiliated institutions have a warm, loving, Christian atmosphere that will support and comfort your parents as they become more frail. If you and they choose carefully, CCRCs can offer a very good living arrangement.

BOARD-AND-CARE HOMES

Briefly, board-and-care homes provide for the needs of ambulatory frail elderly who are not sick enough to require skilled nursing care, but can't be left alone. Residents have a bedroom (private or semi-private—i.e., shared) and common living and dining areas. They receive assistance with taking medications, dressing, bathing, and other necessary functions. Although costs are less than in skilled nursing facilities, they are not inexpensive. (Current monthly charges for board and care can range from $500 to $1500 per month and up.)

Some states license board-and-care homes just as they do nursing homes. In these states, lists of licensed homes should be available from your local agency on aging. In states without licensing, proceed with caution. The same standards and care should be applied in choosing a board-and-care home as in choosing a nursing home. (See chapter 11.)

SHOULD YOUR PARENT LIVE WITH YOU?

A last resort for most elderly people is living with an adult child. The elderly parent can no longer live alone, is not impaired enough to be in a nursing home, and doesn't have the money to live anywhere else. Yet he dreads losing his independence, moving in with his child, and "becoming a burden."

Three-generation households can work wonderfully

well. Grandparents who love children are helpful to have around in a family. They make wonderful babysitters, act as buffers between children and parents, and teach children that older people can be lovable human beings.

Most success stories about Grandma joining the household are about relatively "young old" Grandmas. If Grandma has grown old within an adult child's family, everybody has gradually adjusted to the changes taking place in her. But if Grandma, at age eighty, suddenly moves in after living elsewhere for fifty or more years or if she's frail and perhaps a little confused and needs a lot of help every day, the adjustment process can be traumatic.

The most important questions are "Does she really want to come?" and "Do you really want to have her?" The easiest adjustments are made by people who want to make them. Caregivers who move a parent in to avoid feeling guilty usually find the parent is unhappy, and they end up feeling guilty anyway. If possible, try to leave open a dignified means of exiting from the arrangement if it doesn't work out. Instead of having your parent sell her home and burn all her bridges behind her, consider having her move in for a trial period of several months, after which you'll both evaluate the situation.

If you are contemplating having a parent move into your household, how does your spouse feel about this? Unless you have his or her full support, it isn't going to work. You'll end up having to choose between your spouse and your parent. How do any children still living at home feel? Will they have to make sacrifices—for example, giving up a bedroom? What has their relationship with this older person been like in the past? If it was warm and loving, these good feelings will help everybody through the adjustment period. If not, you'll be caught in the middle between your parent and your children. (See chapter 6 on counting the cost.)

Will your home become a joint household or will your parent become a dependent in your household? In a joint household, both generations contribute financially and share in the workload and decision making. An example would be an elderly widow and an adult daughter who take an apartment together, each bringing some furniture and belongings to the newlyformed household. This is very different from the frail, elderly widow who comes to you as a dependent. If your parent expects to be part of a joint household and you expect her to become a dependent in yours, your vastly different expectations are bound to cause conflict.

Conflict is not a bad thing, unless you lack any means of resolving it. If you've always had to watch what you say around your mother for fear of hurting her feelings, the very air in your home will crackle with the tension of unresolved conflicts.

There are so many things that need to be discussed before an elderly person moves into your home that Christian Caregivers Support Group put together a little brochure called "Before Mom Comes," which outlines some of the questions that will come up. These include the following:

►Does she accept your spouse as head of the house? Is there anyone in your household that she doesn't get along with—including pets?

►Are there differences in lifestyles that will cause conflict—e.g., she loves television and you hate it; she goes to bed and gets up early and you're a night owl?

►Will she be bringing any pets? Who will care for them?

►Will she share in performing household tasks such as cooking and cleaning? How will these responsibilities be decided?

►Will she parent your children, if any are living at home?

►Will she have her own room? Her own furniture and television?

►Will your home require modifications to make it safe for an elderly person—e.g., grab bars in the shower, well-lighted stairs, and no highly waxed floors and throw rugs to cause falls?

►Is she able to take care of her own personal needs—

bathing, dressing, toileting, and taking medications—
or will she require help?

▶Does she like the food you serve or does she require a
special diet? If the latter, will you be expected to cook
two menus, one for her and one for the rest of the
family?

▶What will she do all day long in your home? Does
she have interests she can continue to pursue? If you
are a full-time homemaker, will she expect you to be
her companion? If she has to be alone, will she become
isolated, bored, and depressed?

▶Will her family and friends be able to visit? Will she
be able to visit others; attend church services and
functions, social events, and senior activities; do volunteer work?

▶Will she maintain her car and driver's license? If not,
is other transportation available, or will you have to
become her driver?

▶Will she contribute to household expenses? Will anyone else in the family assist financially?

▶Is she able to manage her own financial affairs? If
not, now or in the future, who will take over this
responsibility?

▶Will you have time alone for you and your spouse,
and for you and your children? How will this be managed without making her feel "left out"? Will you be
able to take vacations without her? What about her
vacations?

▶Is she able to stay by herself while you're away? Is she
willing to?

▶If respite care is needed so you and your spouse can
get away, is there anyone in the family who will provide it? If not, how will you manage to get respite?
Does she understand your need for it, and is she willing
to cooperate so you can have it? If you become ill, who
will take over?

▶Is there a will and a safety deposit box? Where does

she keep important papers?

▶Will she continue with her present physician, or will you have to find a new one for her? Are she and her doctor willing to discuss her medical care with you? Do you know how she feels about life-prolonging treatments? Has she communicated her wishes to her physician?

▶Who will care for her if she becomes ill? Will insurance cover medical and home health care costs and, if necessary, long-term care costs?

▶Do you know her wishes in regard to disposition of her belongings? What about funeral arrangements?

Possible Problem Areas

Most people (myself included) underestimate the changes that take place in the elderly person's body that others in the household must adjust to. The elderly do everything slowly. The difference in the pace of your lives can grate on your nerves.

You may be used to turning down the thermostat to save fuel, but your parent feels the cold more than you do. If you keep the temperature low, she could suffer from hypothermia. Turn it up so she's comfortable, and you're sweating.

Grandma doesn't hear well, so she keeps the radio and television blaring when you'd like peace and quiet. She can't hear a conversation unless someone talks to her one-on-one, so the usual banter around the dinner table leaves her out, and she sulks. She expects three cooked, sit-down meals per day; your family warms food in the microwave and shifts for itself.

She gets tired easily, so if you take her on a family outing, she wants to go home after a half hour while the rest of the family wants to stay and enjoy themselves.

She can't or won't go out to a senior center or pursue her own activities, and you're used to coming and going as you please. Do you stay home and feel resentful or go out and feel guilty?

She has very little to do, so she watches you. (If you're

really unlucky, she'll give you helpful "suggestions" while she's watching.) If you're not used to doing cooking and housework in front of a live audience, this can be unnerving. "I stopped sewing for this reason," said one caregiver. "Her watching made me so nervous that I didn't enjoy it any more."

I hate to sound negative, but when I was a caregiver, the people who told me only how wonderful it was having an older person living with them made me feel inferior and inadequate. I needed to know that I wasn't the only one who found it difficult.

You need flexibility and patience. In some areas you'll have to change. The elderly can't be hurried. In other areas you can compromise. You can't afford to keep your house at 85 degrees all winter, but your parent can dress in warmer clothing.

But in some areas your parent will have to live by your rules. It's not fair, for example, for her to keep her television set blaring late at night when you and your spouse need to sleep. If she refuses to adapt somewhat to your household, you won't be able to continue having her live with you without having a health breakdown.

You will find having an elderly person in your home tremendously challenging. Only the grace of God makes it possible. But if both of you are able to accept and meet these challenges, you'll feel greatly rewarded for making the effort.

IF YOUR PARENT ISN'T HAPPY

I wish I could guarantee that if you follow a prearranged formula, your parent will adjust happily to a new living arrangement. But this just isn't so. Some elderly people transplant well and some don't. Hannah is a ninety-two-year-old lady of pioneering stock who, until two years ago, lived alone on her ranch, miles from the nearest neighbor. Her son John, her caregiver, tells her story:

"The turning point came around age ninety. Mother was hospitalized for ten days for congestive heart failure. Against her doctor's advice and, really, my own best judgment, I took her home.

"I'd go down once a week [a six-hour round trip from his home in the city] and take her to town to do her marketing. I could see she was buying groceries she'd never use, yet she wasn't eating right. She lived on toast, honey, and malted milk. Sometimes she couldn't remember if she'd eaten.

"Every day, old family friends came and checked on Mother and gave feed to her cattle. They could see that the situation was getting worse. But Mother wouldn't think of living anywhere else. She'd come to this ranch as a bride in 1914. It was only five miles from the ranch where she was born that her grandparents had homesteaded in the 1850s. She loved her cows, her chickens, the dogs and cats. The country was all she'd known all her life. That and hard work — up to age ninety, she was still canning and preserving food from the garden the same way she did when the family was home.

"But she wasn't happy at the ranch anymore. She couldn't do the work, and she knew that. She was beginning to be frightened. She told me that two men with a truck had backed into the barn and stolen hay, and that she'd recognized one of them. It was a total fantasy. The man she 'recognized' has been dead for ten years.

"After some real anguish and soul searching with my immediate family and my nieces and nephews and our family friends, I announced that the time had arrived — was, in fact, overdue — for her to leave. We talked for four or five hours, and in the end, she got up and walked out on my arm.

"But she hasn't been happy since! I took her to a board-and-care home in town because I thought she'd at least be near relatives and friends. That lasted a month. It looked nice, but it was too regimented. Now she's in a board-and-care home near me. Every day I hear, 'Why am I here in this prison? When can I go home?' 'What have I done wrong now? Why is God punishing me like this?'

"I feel so guilty. I keep asking myself, 'Did I do the right thing? Is there something more I can do?'"

The answer is no. There really is nothing more that John can do. With the help of family and friends, he kept his mother in her own home for far longer than most people are able to manage. When she could no longer stay—by her paranoia she had expressed her fear of being alone—John moved her to where she's getting the best possible care.

To leave her alone on the ranch would be criminally neglectful. Nor could John take her to live with him. His wife has serious health problems, and he can't take care of both of them. His mother would not be happy in his home anyway. She's made it clear that the only home she'll accept is the ranch.

It's tragic that this formerly strong, hard-working lady could not die with her boots on. But the tragedy is not of John's making, and he's guilty of nothing but loving-kindness toward his mother. It's not his fault that she simply can't adjust to life away from the ranch.

You might ask, "What if I move my mother and she's not happy? I'll feel so guilty." Should you feel guilty? No. You are not responsible for the fact that she's grown old and frail and can no longer take care of herself where she is. Nor are you responsible for how well she adjusts. It's not anybody's fault— least of all yours.

10

Coping with the Health Problems of Aging

My soul is bereft of peace, I have forgotten what happiness is.
Lamentations 3:17, RSV

People now in their late seventies, eighties, and nineties are incredibly tough; to survive before the days of vaccines and antibiotics they had to be. But that doesn't necessarily mean that they're well. Twentieth-century medical science has conquered most of the diseases they survived in their younger days. Now they have to face the illnesses that have not been conquered: heart attacks and strokes, cancer, Parkinson's disease, Alzheimer's disease, and others.

These diseases can be treated (and medical science now thinks, perhaps, prevented), but with the exception of some cancers, they cannot be cured. They are chronic, as opposed to acute diseases (such as pneumonia). With treatment, most patients with chronic diseases can be kept alive for many years. Chronic diseases cause most of your parents' suffering in their old age; and, frequently, the elderly suffer from more than one disease.

That would be difficult enough by itself. But there's more. The elderly suffer from multiple, chronic diseases in a health care system that's geared to the treatment and cure of acute illnesses. Despite the fact that chronic, preventable diseases are the major health problems, medical schools are still training doctors to be warriors in the battle against acute diseases. Most hospitals are acute care hospitals. The result is often poor quality care for the older patient.

Doctors trained in acute care are often uncomfortable with older patients. No matter what these doctors do, their older patients are not going to get well. This is unfortunate because older people in this country see the doctor more often, consume more medicines, and are hospitalized more often than younger persons are. Yet they are less likely to get quality care than are their younger counterparts.

Therefore, you face an enormous challenge in helping your parents cope with health problems. Caregivers need to become their parents' advocates with the health care system. You may need to question a doctor's decisions or demand better care whenever you encounter uncaring hospital or nursing homes staffs. You need to be alert to the possible side effects of drugs that can cause symptoms of dementia or other disease states. Where are you going to learn all that you need to know?

Probably not from doctors. Even the best of them are too busy to do much patient education. The people who know the most about keeping patients functioning and comfortable when they suffer from the chronic diseases of aging are the geriatric nurse, the occupational and physical therapist, the social worker, the psychologist, and the lay people who are active in the nonprofit organizations for various diseases. If you don't learn much from the doctor, ask for referrals to someone who can give you more information.

Such groups as the American Cancer Society, the American Heart Association, the Alzheimer's Disease and Related Disorders Association, the American Parkinson's Disease Association, and others like them help patients and their families learn as much as they can about living with these chronic diseases. By going to local meetings of these organizations, you can learn from the people who are actually coping with these diseases every day. These groups also publish free or low-cost booklets with helpful information for patients and their families. (See Appendix.)

Hospitals and other community groups also sponsor workshops on health concerns of the elderly. If you belong to a caregivers' support group, you can exchange information with other members.

YOUR PARENT'S DOCTOR

Your parent needs to be under the care of a good doctor who will coordinate all her treatment. The doctor in charge may be in geriatrics, internal medicine, or family practice (a general practitioner). She may also need to see specialists — one caregiver took her mother to five different doctors in two weeks. But if one doctor isn't in charge, each specialist will prescribe medication for his area of the body, and your parent will end up taking a collection of medications that can cause worse symptoms than those they were supposed to alleviate.

How involved should you be with your parent's doctor? That may depend on how much involvement your parent and the doctor will allow. If your parent tells the doctor not to discuss her care with you, his hands are tied. Ethically and legally, he cannot talk to you.

Fortunately, most parents won't take that attitude. And most doctors are eager to have the cooperation of family members, recognizing that the family takes most of the responsibility for seeing that their instructions are carried out. If you are taking your parent to her doctor's appointments, you will have the opportunity to follow her into the treatment room and talk to the doctor yourself. But should you? Wouldn't that be an invasion of your parent's privacy?

A great deal will depend on whether or not your parent is mentally alert enough to communicate with the doctor and remember and follow his instructions. If she cannot, it will be helpful for you to make an appointment with your parent's doctor to discuss her health care. (You may have to pay for an office visit, but the peace of mind you receive will be well worth it.)

You may be able to help by writing down your parent's questions so that she's prepared for the visit and by writing down the doctor's instructions as he speaks. Anyone can become confused: "Now, did he say come back in three months or six months? And am I supposed to continue with these pills when I start the new ones or not?" If your parent feels comfortable using a tape recorder, the doctor may be willing to dictate his instructions onto a tape that you or she can play back later.

Many older people, although mentally alert, don't always tell the doctor the whole story. Your parent may give you a blow-by-blow description of her symptoms and then tell the doctor, "Oh, I'm fine."

What can you do to avoid feeling like a tattletale and

contradicting your parent in front of the doctor? One care-giver I know writes a note to the doctor and hands it to the nurse who attaches it to the chart so that the doctor can read it before he sees her mother. Another option is to phone the doctor's office in advance of your parent's visit. The doctor may instruct the office nurse to take down your message and relay it to him before each visit.

Most elderly people don't question "doctor's orders," but you should. When a doctor says, "Nothing can be done," he often means, "There's nothing more *I* can do." Always ask, "Is there someone else who could help?" (He may refer you to a physical therapist, psychologist, registered dietitian, or other specialists.) Also ask, "Is there any other treatment for this condition?" and "Is there any other medication that could be used?" The lay person is usually not aware of alternative treatments. Medical consumers do have choices and the right to weigh the risks against the benefits of each treatment. The doctor is a guide, not an oracle.

The UCLA/USC Long Term Care Gerontology Center publishes a low-cost booklet for older adults called *How to Talk to Your Doctor*. (See the Appendix for ordering information.) Critics of the booklet say it's paternalistic and patronizing. It concentrates on teaching the reader how to be a "good patient"—cooperative and docile, not wasting the doctor's precious time. It says nothing about doctors who are too impatient and rushed to listen to their patients. However, the booklet does have some useful tips, especially the lists of questions to ask when you make your first appointment and during your first visit to a new doctor.

When You Have to Choose a Doctor for a Parent
The time to look for a doctor is before your parent needs one. Begin by compiling a list of names gathered from friends, family, nurses, support groups, and local chapters of public interest groups (such as the organizations listed in the Appendix). Hospital nurses are an especially good source of information—they know and are willing to share a great deal about

doctors' medical skills and personalities.

Narrow down the list by calling the doctors' offices. You may be unpleasantly surprised to learn that some doctors on your list do not accept elderly patients. From those who do, you can obtain the answers to some of your questions over the phone, thus eliminating all but the two or three you will want to interview personally.

The following advice on how to find a doctor is from a workshop given by Leslie Ann Dahm, a private health care consultant in northern California:[1]

1) Find out as much as you can about a doctor's training. Where did he do his residency? What are his credentials? (Board certification in his specialty is best.) What hospitals is he currently affiliated with?

2) What is his age? Older is not necessarily better. Younger doctors' training is more recent, and they may have a lower patient load.

3) Is he in group practice or alone? Doctors in group practice are more able to take time off for continuing education. If he is not in a group practice, who covers for him when he's gone?

4) Does he keep up with advances in medicine? What were the most recent courses or seminars that he took?

5) What are his office hours? Are they convenient for you? What's the average wait when you have an appointment? What time does the doctor arrive in the morning? (Beware of the doctor who books patients beginning at nine but arrives at ten!)

6) Does he return phone calls fairly promptly?

7) Will his staff submit insurance claims? Does he take Medicare assignment? If not, what are his fees?

8) What is his practice environment like? You will be spending a lot of time with the people who work for the doctor. Are they courteous and caring? How are you treated over the phone? (You will, of course, learn more about the office staff and the general atmosphere

of the office by visiting.) Dahm advises that you set up interviews with the doctors you're considering, offering to pay for an office visit.

I would add that you should take your parent to the doctor's office and observe how he treats her. Does he talk to you and ignore her? Does the doctor really listen to her? To you? His nonverbal behavior will tell you more about whether he really likes and respects old people than his words will. It's also important that your parent like him. If she doesn't like and trust the doctor, I can guarantee that she won't cooperate in following his treatment plan.

A very important question to ask the doctor is "If my parent has to be in a board-and-care home or nursing home, will you visit her there?" If the answer is no, this could become a very big future problem.

Do you feel comfortable asking this doctor questions?

"You must tell the doctor if you don't understand," Dahm says. "Women are raised to be pleasers. We think it's impolite to ask too many questions. When the doctor acts impatient, we feel dumb and intimidated.

"Tell yourself, 'I am not rambling. I have the right to ask questions and get answers.' Don't be afraid to be labeled a 'difficult patient.' It could save your life."

DRUGS AND THE AGING BODY

It's normal for all bodily functions to slow down with age. This includes the liver and kidneys, two organs that rid the body of toxic substances, including medicines. The older person can't handle as large a dose of medicine as a younger person can because his organs can't get rid of it as fast. So it builds up in his system and poisons him.

Some of the symptoms of this toxicity include zombielike behavior, sluggishness and sleepiness, slurred speech, depression, agitation, and nervousness. Some doctors will treat these symptoms with additional drugs, thereby making matters worse. Many supposedly senile elderly people are actually suffering from drug overdoses.

The danger of adverse drug reaction is increased when seniors take multiple medications. Some drugs are antagonistic and work against each other when taken together. Others are synergistic; one multiplies the effect of the other when taken together. Some drugs taken for one medical condition will worsen another. This is true for over-the-counter as well as prescription drugs. Even such "harmless" drugstore remedies as aspirin, cold and allergy pills, or antacids can have ill effects on those who suffer from high blood pressure, glaucoma, and other conditions that often afflict the elderly.[2]

If you suspect that your parent's symptoms are caused by his medication, never tell him to stop taking it on his own. Patients must be eased off many drugs carefully under a doctor's supervision. Stopping suddenly could be harmful or even fatal.

The confused elderly sometimes take medications incorrectly—they either forget them altogether or forget they've already taken them and take too much. A little device that you can buy in most drugstores holds a week's supply of pills in compartments labeled for each day. But sometimes the elderly take so many drugs—some of which must be taken with food, some without—that you may need to make a wall chart for your parent, showing what pills to take when, with spaces to check off when he's done so. If you don't know which pills need to be taken with food, your pharmacist can tell you. Your pharmacist can also remove on request those pesky childproof caps on pill bottles that are so hard for the elderly to get off (unless they need to protect visiting children).

If it's difficult even for doctors to keep up with new medications and their side effects, no wonder it's confusing for the lay person. It seldom occurs to most people to ask their pharmacist, but these professionals are more knowledgeable about drugs than most doctors, since drugs are their specialty. It's often advantageous to take all your prescriptions to the same place, since some pharmacies now keep computerized records of all the drugs a person is taking. They should be able to alert you to possible adverse drug interactions. If you want a reference for home use, buy the *Physicians Desk Reference* (also available secondhand and in most public libraries' reference departments).

But this is written for the physician, not the lay person, and isn't easy reading. Instead, I recommend *50+: The Graedons' People's Pharmacy for Older Adults* by Joe and Teresa Graedon, along with their earlier book, *The People's Pharmacy*. The Graedons are pharmacists who write simply and understandably. *50+*, in addition to alerting you to drug dangers, has helpful chapters on how to take medicine, a sample medication chart, tips on how to save money when buying drugs, and other vital matters. (Other books are listed in the Appendix.)

Don't Accept "Old Age" as a Diagnosis

It isn't easy to know when a parent's health problems are the result of normal aging and when they're the result of some disease process. But doctors are frequently too quick to blame "old age" for everything. It's not always because they're uninterested in the elderly. Often a diagnosis is missed because older people's symptoms are atypical. Depression is one example. Another reason is that many of the symptoms of chronic diseases begin slowly. But sometimes the doctor dismisses a complaint that could be treated as "old age" out of ignorance.

Incontinence is a good example of one such failed diagnosis. When it occurs, the older person is so embarrassed that she begins to withdraw from social situations. It's also one of the greatest difficulties for families to manage at home and can result in a parent being placed in a nursing home before it's really necessary. Often the older patient, believing that nothing can be done and suffering from a deep sense of shame, tries to hide the problem. It's estimated that only one of twelve adults suffering from incontinence seeks help.

Yet from 85 to 90 percent of incontinence is treatable, according to Dr. David R. Staskin, a urologist at the Boston

University School of Medicine. The first step for your parent should be a physical examination by her physician. If he says he can't help her, ask for a referral to a urologist or contact one of the organizations listed in the Appendix.

There are different types of incontinence—overflow, stress, urge, and reflex—and each has different treatments, ranging from exercises to strengthen the sphincter muscles to behavior modification and bladder retraining, medication, and surgery. Even nursing home patients have been able to reduce their incidents of incontinence through training with behavior modification methods.

UNDERSTANDING SOME CHRONIC DISEASES IN THE AGING

Alzheimer's Disease and Other Dementias

In 1986, an estimated 2.5 million people had Alzheimer's disease. That's a lot of sufferers, yet Alzheimer's afflicts only from seven to nine percent of the population. Alzheimer's disease cannot be cured or reversed at present, but other dementias (mental impairment) that are not caused by Alzheimer's *are* reversible. A thorough examination by a neurologist and/or psychiatrist or psychologist is vital to rule out other causes. (Often a team approach is used at large medical centers.)

Alzheimer's devastating effect on families can't be measured by mere numbers. All dementias begin with forgetfulness and confusion, but Alzheimer's progresses to a complete mental and physical breakdown, ending in death. The ability to think and plan goes; the personality changes; victims no longer remember how to dress, bathe, feed, and toilet themselves; eventually, they become unable to communicate or recognize others. The disease may progress rapidly or slowly over a period of years.

The victim becomes a stranger to his family. He may become anxious and agitated, hostile and aggressive. He may become negative, like a two-year-old. He may wander away and get lost. He may stay awake all night. He may lose the brain functions that inhibit socially unacceptable behavior. Many patients develop a fear of water, and getting them to bathe can become an ordeal. (Behavior modification techniques used by a trained professional sometimes can overcome this problem.)

Even if a dementia can't be cured, it can be treated by making adjustments in the patient's environment. Many large university medical centers have memory clinics that take a team approach to helping victims of memory loss and their families. For example, at U.C.-Irvine in Southern California, patients are tested, then evaluated by a team of neurologists, psychologists, and therapists. They then make recommendations to the patient's caregiver, sometimes sending an occupational therapist to the home to make suggestions for adapting his surroundings.

Drug companies are pouring money into research on drugs to restore memory, and many experts believe researchers are close to a breakthrough. However, Dr. Arnold Starr, chairman of the Department of Neurology at U.C.-Irvine is skeptical: "I think you'll get more benefit from lifestyle changes—the things you do yourself—than any drugs doctors will be able to prescribe."

The Alzheimer's patient needs twenty-four-hour-per-day supervision, and the caregiver must have help. The environment needs to be structured to reduce confusion, with everything in the home kept in a consistent place, all dangerous things locked up, and a strict daily routine followed. Taking the patient for walks often reduces agitation and helps him sleep at night. Where available, day-care centers not only give respite to the caregiver but provide the patient with much-needed socialization on his own level. Usually, in the final stages of the disease, nursing home care becomes a necessity.

There are so many techniques to be learned in managing the mentally impaired older adult that it's impossible to summarize them here. Communication with these patients works best on an emotional level, through their feelings, and by nonverbal expressions of caring like hugging, patting, and listening (even if they don't make sense). Confrontations and arguments should be avoided.

Those who work with Alzheimer's patients have a special calling. Said Linda Fodrini, who runs a day-care center for dementia sufferers: "It's not depressing to me. These people live in the moment. They have no past, so they have no guilt. They have no future, so they have no anxiety about tomorrow. If I can make this present moment happy for them, I've accomplished a great deal."

Several helpful books are listed in the Appendix. Support groups and day-care centers specifically for the families of brain-impaired elders can be located through the Alzheimer's Disease and Related Disorders Association.

Arthritis

A chronic disease that affects the joints, muscles, and connective tissues of the body, arthritis has many different forms. The most common in older people is osteoarthritis. Symptoms are pain and stiffness and range from mild in severity to severe and disabling.

Although it can't be cured, arthritis can be treated through adaptive techniques to protect the joints from strain and to keep them moving. Unless joints and muscles are moved daily, they can become frozen and useless. Many local Arthritis Foundation chapters sponsor water exercise classes. Since no strain is placed on the joints under water, they can be moved more freely.

Other treatments include hot and cold applications and medication to reduce pain and inflammation. As a last resort, there is joint-replacement surgery.

Coping with this disease will place your parent under emotional stress. Support groups that help patients live with chronic pain and stress are sponsored by local Arthritis Foundation chapters and some hospitals. Booklets are published by the Foundation on arthritis self-care, coping with pain, and other topics. (See Appendix.) The pain booklet has a number of helpful tips on nondrug methods of relieving pain. You should be aware that aspirin and nonsteroidal anti-inflammatory drugs (NSAIDS) can cause stomach bleeding and ulcers.

Bronchitis/Emphysema

Two lung diseases that sometimes occur in the older years are chronic bronchitis and emphysema. In bronchitis, airways in the lungs become narrow and clogged with mucus. In emphysema, air sacs deep in the lungs are damaged. Symptoms are coughing, wheezing, and shortness of breath, all of which interfere with the sufferer's daily activities. The majority of sufferers are men who were heavy smokers.

Since there is no cure for the damaged lungs, patients have to be educated in how to live with these diseases. Therapy includes training in relaxation, breathing techniques, clearing the lungs of mucus, general conditioning exercises, and medications. Bronchodilators in the form of pills, liquids, and sprays are often prescribed to open up clogged airways. Nebulizers are sprayers that deliver a mist of medicine deep into the lungs. Breathing machines use pressure to force air deep into the lungs. Sometimes oxygen is prescribed. Either the patient or the caregiver or both must be trained in the use of this equipment.

Being unable to breathe is frightening. So is watching a loved one struggle for breath. It helps if you can talk to your parent about these feelings. In order to cope, the sufferer from bronchitis and emphysema must learn to help himself, and a number of hospitals provide patient education programs and support groups to help him. Another resource is your local chapter of the American Lung Association.

High Blood Pressure

High blood pressure is not a disease *per se*. But because it is a major cause of heart attacks, strokes, and kidney failure, yet causes no symptoms, doctors monitor blood pressure carefully and use various medications in attempting to bring it down. Some doctors also restrict their patients' intake of salt.

However, many people being treated for high blood pressure don't really have it. They become anxious and their blood pressure shoots up in the doctor's office. If you suspect this might be the case with your parent, ask the doctor to remeasure her, or take her to be remeasured in another setting. You can also buy home devices for measuring blood pressure.

So many older people are on blood pressure medications that you need to be aware of these drugs and their side effects. If your parent is on blood pressure medication, she will have to continue taking it for life; her pressure will stay down only as long as she takes her pills.

Doctors usually first treat their older patients with diuretics (such as chlorothiazide, chlorthalidone, Dyazide, and Lasix), which work by stimulating urination, forcing fluids out of the body and reducing the volume of blood. But they also deplete the body's potassium, leading to dizziness and weakness, and may increase cholesterol and blood sugar levels. Some medication gets around the potassium problem by combining a diuretic with potassium supplements. If your parent's medicine does not contain potassium, she needs to eat potassium-rich foods, such as oranges, bananas, cantaloupe, and baked potatoes.

Don't ignore dizziness or weakness in an older person on diuretics. Report the symptoms to the doctor, who should be monitoring your parent's potassium level with blood tests as long as she's on this medication.

A second large class of medications for high blood pressure is beta blockers (Inderal, Capoten, Vasotec, and others), which reduce the heart rate and the output of blood from the heart. These powerful medications are notorious for causing depression. They can also cause joint pain, which mimics arthritis and asthma and results in sleep disorders, mental confusion, forgetfulness, impotence in males, and other disorders. If your parent experiences any of these conditions, suspect the medication. But warn her not to stop taking the pills without consulting her physician. Sudden withdrawal of beta blockers can cause a heart attack.

A newer group of medications called calcium channel blockers (Cardizem, Calan, Isoptin, Adalat, Procardia) has recently come onto the market. They seem to lower blood pressure with few if any side effects.

Cancer

Probably no diagnosis strikes such fear into the heart as cancer. But if discovered and treated early, the possibility of cure is excellent. Remember, though, that in your parent's youth, cancer was an unmentionable disease, a death sentence. She may still react to her diagnosis with fear and shame. If your parent has cancer, she will not only need assistance in some of the tasks of daily living, but also a great deal of emotional support.

Despite the number of people who live for years when they're given "two months to live," doctors still hand out these death sentences. Remind your parent that miraculous recoveries as the result of prayer are well known. (Skeptical medical science, which has to call them something, calls them "spontaneous remissions.")

Should your parent be told that she has cancer? Most people believe it is her right to know. Attempting to live a lie in the final part of her life will strain your relationship and deny both of you the comfort of saying good-by.

Your local branch of the American Cancer Society (ACS) can provide a great deal of help: counseling for you or your parent in what to expect and what kinds of assistance are available, the loan of hospital-type equipment for the home (hospital beds, wheelchairs, etc.), surgical dressings, transportation to medical appointments, and rehabilitation services. I Can Cope is an educational course given by the ACS in many hospitals. All of these services are free.

Diabetes

Diabetes is the nation's third leading cause of death. In this disease, a form of sugar called glucose accumulates in the blood instead of providing energy for the body. Insulin, a hormone produced by the pancreas, converts sugar into energy. In Type I diabetes, which usually begins early in life, the pancreas does not manufacture insulin. In Type II diabetes, which occurs most often in overweight people over forty, the pancreas either doesn't make enough insulin or the body is unable to use the insulin being produced. Ninety percent of all diabetics, ten million Americans, have Type II diabetes.

Even a slight loss of weight increases the body's ability to use the insulin that it produces. Your parent's doctor will treat his Type II diabetes first with diet and exercise. If that does not bring down blood sugar levels, the doctor will probably prescribe oral medication such as Diabanese to lower his blood sugar.

Many families may not realize the very serious consequences of diabetes. Elevated blood sugar levels damage blood vessels and nerves, and elderly people can become blind or require the amputation of feet or legs as a complication of this disease.

When the blood vessels in the back of the eyes are damaged, the diabetic's vision is threatened. Since this can be treated if discovered in the early stages, diabetics should be seen frequently by an ophthalmologist. When blood vessels in the legs are damaged, this interferes with blood circulation and slows healing of any injuries. Damage to the nerves in the legs causes numbness and loss of feeling. Minor injuries to the feet and legs can become badly infected before they're discovered. Diabetics must take good care of their feet every day. Damage to blood vessels and nerves also leads to impotence in males. Also, diabetics, because they may have damaged blood vessels, become more susceptible to kidney disease, heart attacks, and strokes.

Unfortunately, symptoms of diabetes come on slowly, and the disease may go undetected for years. Meanwhile, blood vessels and nerves are irreparably damaged. Once diagnosed, diabetes has to be monitored carefully by the patient or his caregiver. Type II diabetics must test their own blood sugar levels every day.

Diabetics whose blood sugar gets too high could lapse into a coma. Diabetics who take oral medicine may suffer from hypoglycemia (too low a level of blood sugar). Unless they promptly eat something high in sugar content, they could pass out. This is extremely dangerous in older people who may injure themselves or be misdiagnosed as suffering from a stroke. For this reason, encourage your diabetic parent to wear an I.D. bracelet at all times and a Lifeline (a device electronically connected to a hospital) while at home.

The American Diabetes Association publishes a booklet called "Seniors: Diabetes and You" that contains basic diabetes information, as well as specific leaflets on eye care, foot care, and other topics. These are free. They also sell cookbooks and meal planning guides specifically for diabetics. (See Appendix.)

Heart Disease/Strokes
These are the leading causes of death in the United States. In a heart attack, heart muscles do not receive enough oxygen and die. In a stroke, parts of the brain do not receive enough oxygen and die. Many heart attacks and strokes are caused by thickened and hardened arteries.

Patients suffering from heart disease can be helped by several surgical procedures: valve replacement, installation of pacemakers, coronary artery bypass grafts, and others. Lasers are being used by some surgeons to remove plaque from clogged arteries.

Drugs are also used to treat hearts that are not receiving the blood, and therefore the oxygen, that they need. These include digitalis, nitroglycerin, and vasodilators. All of these medications can have side effects, such as nausea, dizziness, and weakness, that caregivers need to be aware of.

Many elderly people suffer from congestive heart failure. When this happens, a heart damaged by high blood pressure, heart attack, or arteriosclerosis is not strong enough to keep the blood circulating normally throughout the body. So the blood backs up, causing congestion and swelling in the tissues. This causes the swollen ankles that you often see in the elderly. Fluid can also collect in the lungs, causing shortness of breath. Doctors usually treat congestive heart failure with diuretics to remove the excess fluid.

The American Heart Association's "Heart Facts" booklet, updated yearly, provides the most recent information on heart diseases, treatments, and research.

Strokes occur when a blood vessel carrying oxygen to the brain bursts or becomes clogged with a blood clot. Deprived of oxygen, the brain cells die. The more damage that occurs to the brain, the more disabling the stroke. If the stroke occurs in the left hemisphere of the brain, the patient's right side may be paralyzed. Damage to the right hemisphere of the brain causes paralysis of the left side of the body. Vision, speech, and other brain functions may also be affected.

Stroke patients need rehabilitation as soon as possible after a stroke in order to recover as much of their former functioning as they can. A stroke victim is often referred to a rehabilitation center or sent to a nursing home for rehabilitation.

Families play an enormous role in the recovery of stroke victims, according to the American Heart Association, but they need help in understanding what the patient is going through. The hardest thing is to find a middle ground between expecting too much of the stroke victim, frustrating both him and yourself, and expecting too little, which discourages him from helping himself.

Personality changes in the patient are especially hard to deal with. A patient with left-brain injury is likely to have problems with speech and language (aphasia). A lot of his "uncooperativeness" is lack of understanding. He also tends to be slow, cautious, and disorganized. A patient with right-brain damage will have difficulty judging distance, size, and his own position and rate of movement in space. He tends to be impulsive and rash. Stroke victims sometimes cry or laugh for no apparent reason and have problems with memory, retention span, and generalization.

While the stroke victim is struggling to regain some of what he's lost, his loved ones are struggling with their own emotions. Foremost is the desire to have "the old Dad" back, but this seldom happens. He may get better but "the old Dad" won't be back.

A team approach is needed, involving doctors, nurses, physical therapists, speech therapists, and occupational therapists, but the patient's motivation does most to determine the outcome. Caregivers need to be encouragers. To help them, the American Heart Association publishes "Strokes: A Guide for the Family," "Stroke: Why Do They Behave that Way?" and "Aphasia and the Family," as well as other leaflets (see Appendix).

Osteoporosis
This is not a killer disease—directly—but it leads to falls that can kill or disable its elderly victims. Their bones may become so thin that they crack or break under the slightest pressure. We often say, "Mrs. Smith fell and broke her hip," when what actually happened was that Mrs. Smith's hip broke and then she fell.

Osteoporosis is the cause of the "dowager's hump." The disease affects one woman in four by age sixty and half of all women over eighty. Most victims are small and thin, from northern European or Asian background. There is no cure and very little treatment available.

Your elderly parent may first be diagnosed with osteoporosis when she suffers excruciating pain, often in the back. This is caused by hairline fractures. Eventually they heal, but new ones may occur. A back brace is often prescribed to promote healing and prevent more breaks.

The doctor may prescribe calcium supplements, but there is some controversy over how well they're absorbed into the system. Some doctors also prescribe estrogen, which helps protect women against bone loss. Drugs that seem to reverse bone loss are now being tested, but they're still unproved.

Parkinson's Disease

An estimated 500,000 people—one person in 500 over the age of fifty—suffer from Parkinson's, a disease in which an area of cells in the middle part of the brain controlling movement, posture, balance, and walking degenerates and dies.

In addition to the characteristic muscular tremor, stiffness of muscles, and loss of balance, the disease can also affect the autonomous nervous system, resulting in drooling, forced eyelid closure, and difficulty in breathing. Less common symptoms are dementia, short-term memory loss, a "masked" facial expression, decreased blinking/increased staring, loss of vocal power, and difficulties in speaking and swallowing, among others.

Life for the Parkinson's patient becomes increasingly difficult as slowness of movement interferes with eating, dressing, and toileting. The loss of balance places him in constant danger of falling. Unless he's determined to stay active and follow an exercise program, joints will freeze and unused muscles will shrink until movement becomes more and more difficult. Treatment consists of drugs, physical therapy, and home exercises to keep muscles and joints functioning as long as possible. Speech therapy can also help patients who experience difficulty in speaking.

The drug most used to treat Parkinson's is L-Dopa (Senimet). Unfortunately, it is not well tolerated by all patients and tends to lose its effectiveness with time.[3]

The most important element in coping with Parkinson's is the patient's attitude. Tension and anxiety may worsen the symptoms. Anything you as a caregiver can do to encourage a positive attitude in your parent and find substitutes for the activities he must give up will be helpful. Many of the mobility aids in *The Gadget Book* can also be used by Parkinson's patients. A Parkinson's support group may help by providing him with emotional support and coping skills.

The American Parkinson's Disease Association has information and referral centers throughout the United States, usually located near universities and medical schools. It also publishes a number of booklets, including "Parkinson's Disease Handbook," "A Manual for Patients with Parkinson's Disease," "Aids, Equipment and Suggestions to Help the Patient with Parkinson's Disease in the Activities of Daily Living," and "Home Exercises for Patients with Parkinson's Disease." (See Appendix.)

WHAT IF YOUR PARENT WON'T COOPERATE?

Diet, exercise, and medication are important to the treatment of most of these chronic diseases, but what if your parent won't cooperate?

Don't frustrate yourself by falling for the notion that you're responsible for your parent's health. The reality is that every mentally-competent person, no matter how old, is in charge of his own health. If your dad won't exercise, you can't make him. If your diabetic mother wants to cheat and eat candy, she'll find a way to do it. Make it clear to them that it's their choice, then let go. Whatever happens, you're not responsible. Besides, they're much more likely to comply if you step back and treat them like adults than if you nag and scold them like naughty children.

THE HOSPITALIZED ELDERLY

Hospitalization of a parent presents additional challenges for the caregiver. Writing in *Generations*, the journal of the American Society on Aging, Lawrence Z. Rubenstein, M.D., associate professor of geriatric medicine at UCLA Medical School, says:

"[T]he elderly have not fared as well in hospitals as have younger people. Mortality rates are higher, lengths of stay longer, complications more frequent, use of emergency rather than elective surgery more common . . . . [A] substantial part of this discrepancy is avoidable and relates to inadequate diagnosis and treatment, quite possibly a result of agist approaches to medical care."[4]

Most nurses and hospital workers are caring people, but they're also busy people. Even when they don't share society's prejudices against the elderly, they may be too rushed to take the time to communicate with elderly patients. Mrs. King doesn't respond; therefore, she must be senile. But Mrs. King doesn't hear well. Did anyone take the time to find this out and to talk to her reassuringly, slowly, and distinctly, face to face, so she could hear?

Many elderly patients do exhibit symptoms of "senility" when hospitalized. As soon as they're home among familiar surroundings, their minds clear. It's up to the family to interpret the elderly patient's needs to the hospital staff and to monitor care, including the drugs given. (Sometimes the "senility" is the result of the hospital's over-medication.) Don't be afraid to ask for what your parent needs, whether it's an egg crate mattress to prevent bedsores or a snack at bedtime.

Medicare regulations to cut hospital costs have resulted in patients being discharged "quicker and sicker." Medicare pays hospitals on DRGs (diagnostically related groups), meaning it pays for the average length of stay for the main complaint for which the patient is hospitalized. If your parent needs a longer stay for her particular case, or if she has multiple complaints, she may be discharged anyway—unless the family complains to the doctor—because the hospital knows it may not get paid for the entire hospital stay.

Be sure to discuss the help your parent will need after discharge with the hospital's discharge planner. Will she be able to cope at home? Will you? Will Medicare or your private insurance (including long-term care policies) pay for home health care? If you have to perform certain nursing procedures at home, who will train you to do this?

SHOULD YOU BE THE NURSE?

If you have to work outside the home, nursing your parent yourself may be impossible. Even if you are at home, should you do this? Do you have a talent for nursing? Some people don't. Does your parent want you to nurse him? What about the modesty issue, particularly with a parent of the opposite sex? There is a great deal to learn about handling a bed-bound patient so that you do not hurt the patient or yourself. If you want to do this, or you feel you have no choice (there is no one else available), home health care courses are given by American Red Cross chapters, county health departments, and some community colleges.

OPPORTUNITIES TO EXERCISE FAITH

It's easy to have faith when everything is going well. But real faith means trusting in God when everything, including even your own body, seems to be falling apart. This is the challenge to their faith that your parents face in old age.

You surely want to encourage your parents to exercise their faith, yet at the same time you don't want to discourage them from expressing their honest feelings. If they complain and you say, "How can you talk like that? Where's your faith?" they will feel alone and abandoned with their "unacceptable" feelings.

Many "unacceptable" feelings occur during illness. Your parents' emotional reactions may range from anxiety and fear to anger, hostility, rage, shame, apathy, depression, and more.

Linda Kinrade, R.N., and Carol Collins, M.F.C.C. (Marriage, Family, and Child Counselor), minister through the Chronic and Critical Illness Christian Counseling Center.[5] Carol has had cancer surgery three times and has a heart pacemaker. Linda is an oncology (cancer) nurse and teaches nursing at a state university.

One of the things that makes illness such a terrifying experience, they believe, is that most people know so little about how their bodies work. Doctors may give information, but patients don't have the background needed to assimilate it. You can help your parents by finding out as much as you can about their illnesses and how they should expect their bodies to react, both to the illness and to the treatment. Often, they need reassurance that what they're experiencing is normal, under the circumstances.

They may feel (especially during hospitalization) that they've become a "thing" that doctors and nurses do various invasive, humiliating, and painful things to. They've lost all control, it seems, even of their own bodies. This may cause them to lose their sense of identity and self-worth. Because diseases such as cancer have often been considered unacceptable, while others such as Parkinson's cause socially unacceptable behavior, patients can come to feel unaccepted and unwanted.

Family support can counteract some of this depersonalization by reminding your parents that they are still loved and important to others, and therefore still persons, not things. Touching tells them they are still connected without your saying a word. They may need to vent their emotions; now is the time to put to use all the active listening skills you learned in chapter 3.

Spiritual Helps During Illness

You will, of course, pray for your parents, and if they permit it, pray with them. What should you pray for? Certainly, pray for healing. God's healing power has no age limitations. But sometimes healing is not to be. The decline in the physical body that leads to death is a natural process, and a necessary one if we're to be raised to eternal life.

Pray that God will be with your parent, that He will strengthen him through this ordeal, that He will comfort him and fill him with His love. Read the Bible to your parent, especially the passages that speak of God's love and comfort of His people.

Often there will appear to be little or no response. But even when the body is incapable of response, your parent's spirit is still present. Even patients in comas or under anesthesia on an operating table can hear what's being said. Now is the time to exercise your faith and believe that your prayers and Bible reading do make a difference, even when there's no evidence for it whatsoever.

Often patients are too weak to concentrate on prayer. But they can keep a single verse of Scripture before them, repeating it and drawing strength and comfort from it all day long. So Carol and Linda give their clients "comfort verses" of Scripture. Their favorite comfort verses include:

▶ "The LORD will fight for you; you need only to be still" (Exodus 14:14).
▶ "But those who hope in the LORD will renew their strength. They will soar on wings like eagles; they will run and not grow weary, they will walk and not be faint" (Isaiah 40:31).
▶ "My God is my rock, in whom I take refuge. He is my shield . . . my stronghold" (Psalm 18:2).
▶ "For I am the LORD, your God, who takes hold of your right hand and says to you, Do not fear; I will help you" (Isaiah 41:13).

You can take one of these or any other of the great messages of affirmation from the Scripture, print it in large letters, and put it where your parent can see it from his bed or wheelchair. You, the doctors and nurses, and all who enter the room will see it, too. It will help all of you.

As you seek comfort from the Scripture for your parent, may the Lord of all comfort you from His Word.

NOTES: 1. Leslie Ann Dahm, 122 Hartford Rd., Danville, CA 94526.
2. The Assembly Office of Research, State of California, found that in 1986, 62 percent of adverse drug reactions reported by hospitals involved patients sixty and older. Nationally, 243,000 older Americans were hospitalized in 1985 because of adverse drug reactions.
3. As we go to press, a new drug called Deprenyl has been introduced for the treatment of Parkinson's.
4. Lawrence Z. Rubenstein, "Innovations in Hospital Care for Elders," *Generations*, journal of the American Society on Aging, Fall 1987, page 65.
5. Chronic and Critical Illness Christian Counseling Center, 2303 Ygnacio Valley Rd., Walnut Creek, CA 94598.

11

When Your Parent Must Be in a Nursing Home

"When you were younger, you dressed yourself and went where you wanted; but when you are old you will stretch out your hands, and someone else will dress you and lead you where you do not want to go."
John 21:18

Fear of nursing homes has become part of our culture. All of us have read newspaper articles about nursing home abuses, or we know somebody who has told us horror stories. Perhaps we've visited nursing homes and witnessed inferior care or callous treatment.

Nothing causes more guilt in families than the decision to place loved ones in a nursing home. The elderly live in dread of them. Many have extracted promises from their families never to put them in one, promises that families sometimes cannot keep.

"I never tell people my mother is in a nursing home," said Anita, a Michigan caregiver. "I dread getting those raised eyebrows or remarks like, 'I would never put my mother away.' It hurts so much! People just don't understand."

Nursing home abuses do exist, but there are also positive aspects to nursing homes. If you can no longer care for your parent properly at home and a nursing home can, then placing a parent in a nursing home is the loving thing to do.

When families choose a nursing home carefully, visit often, monitor the care that's given, and communicate with the administration and staff, there is little likelihood of abuse. In placing your parent in a nursing home, you are not abandoning her, but you are letting go of your control of her care. You have to trust God to take care of what you can no longer do yourself, and that can be difficult.

THE POSITIVE RESULTS OF LETTING GO

Letting go does not mean learning to become indifferent. It means coming to terms with the reality of the nursing home situation. A busy staff will not be able to give your parent the same one-on-one care that you did at home. On the other hand, a nursing home is often able to give your parent what you cannot—the attention of many different staff members, physical therapy, planned activities, and social stimulation.

Of course, it's not the same as being at home. Patients'

lives are regimented; they're told when to get up, when to go to bed, when and what to eat. But sometimes your parents will find security in this regimentation.

You hear a lot of stories about old people who go into decline when they are institutionalized. But some people who enter nursing homes gain something.

Addie struggled to keep her mother walking while keeping her mother in her home, despite the pain of severe arthritis. In the nursing home, the staff didn't do this, and her mother lost her mobility. However, with the encouragement of the activities director, Addie's mother, a talented artist, began painting again. She had never painted while she was living with Addie. Some of her paintings have won awards. Is she better off continuing to walk but not painting, or painting from a wheelchair?

You seldom hear about the people who improve after they enter a nursing home. Henrietta agonized over putting her mother, who was in the latter stages of Parkinson's disease, in a nursing home. But Henrietta's health was failing and she could not go on. When an unexpected opening occurred in a nursing home near her mother's old home, it seemed like a sign from God. Placing her mother there was torture; she almost ran back the same day and took her mother out. But to her amazement, her depressed, apathetic mother perked up and was better than she'd been at home.

Henrietta's mother had been bored and lonely in Henrietta's home. But in the nursing home, there were lots of people to talk to, and her sweet nature made her a favorite of the staff. Before, she'd hardly responded to Henrietta; now she was a joy to visit.

IS GOD PRESENT IN NURSING HOMES?

Too many Christians (and their families) act as if the nursing home bears a sign on the door that reads, "Abandon hope, all ye who enter here." If you truly believe that God is everywhere, then He is surely as present in nursing homes as He is in your own home. God will not abandon your parent at the door of the nursing home; He's going right in there with her.

Harold, eighty-five, was a depressed, apathetic nursing home resident until his pastor reminded him of God's presence. Harold was complaining about how awful it was to be in such a place. "You know," said his pastor, "as a Christian, you can make a difference wherever you are."

Harold took this to heart. He began wheeling himself around in his wheelchair, looking for other residents who needed cheering, telling them about the Lord Jesus, and sharing the love of God. Today everybody in that home has been touched by Harold's ministry. Nothing in Harold's living situation has changed, but he changed when he realized that God was there with him.

CAREGIVERS MUST ADJUST, TOO

If patients need to adjust to being in a nursing home, families, especially caregivers, need to adjust, too.

Before suffering a stroke about a year ago, eighty-eight-year-old Marion had been living with her daughter, Elaine, a single retired teacher. They had always been close, and when Marion's health began to fail, Elaine thought she'd be able to care for her. But the stroke changed everything.

Marion's right side became paralyzed, and she became incontinent. She could no longer feed herself, walk, stand, or get out of bed unaided. To avoid bedsores, she had to be turned in bed every two hours, day and night. It took two people to move her without hurting her. The doctor told Elaine that it would be out of the question for her to care for Marion at home. Elaine had to find a good nursing home fast.

There's so much to consider in choosing a nursing home. But often the move follows a crisis, when you're emotionally upset. Everything you've ever heard about nursing home abuses goes through your head, adding to your fears and anxieties. In choosing a nursing home, you're taking an enormous responsibility for someone else's life. It's easy to become paralyzed by your conflicting emotions—yet you must act.

Despite her emotional turmoil, Elaine got a list of accredited nursing homes from her county Area Agency on Aging. She also sought recommendations from friends and from her mother's doctor. The skilled nursing facility that she chose is a relatively small one, privately owned, near her home and near a large hospital. It offered therapy for her mother's rehabilitation following her stroke. And her mother's doctor would continue to visit her there. The atmosphere is warm, the food is good, the staff is caring, and the nursing supervisor has a reputation for "running a tight ship." A year later, Elaine is happy with her choice.

Yet her adjustment period is not over.

At first, Elaine's major concern was that Marion was not eating nor responding to therapy. At that point, she still hoped her mother would recover sufficiently to be able to come home. But Marion was so terrified of falling that she was afraid to try to walk. The attempts at rehabilitation did not succeed.

Elaine went twice a day to feed her mother, at noon and 5:00 p.m. She was joined by her brother for the evening meal. She felt she was able to coax more food into her mother than the busy staff. At the same time, she agonized over what she saw. Why wasn't there more improvement? Was the staff doing enough? Was there anything more she could do? What should she say when her mother asked to come home?

Over a period of months, Elaine has had to come to terms that her mother's condition is not going to change. Her mother can sit in a wheelchair, but not without slumping over. Her appetite has improved. She's become attached to the aide who cares for her. She asks to go home less often.

When caregivers surrender their loved ones to a nursing home, the process of adjustment is a form of mourning. Elaine goes home to an empty house filled with her mother's things, constant reminders of her loss. Getting rid of them while her mother is still alive is unthinkable to her. She's learning to live with the pain, as well as learning to live alone again.

Many people have told Elaine that twice a day is too often for her to go to the nursing home. Nursing home staffs discourage too-frequent visitation because they believe it makes the patient's adjustment more difficult. But who is to say? This is such an individual matter. I suspect that Elaine will decide in her own way and in her own time what's best for her. Gradually, she has been letting go more and more—for example, she allowed the staff to handle a tender area on her mother's body that's threatening to become a bedsore rather than involving herself in the treatment. She's beginning now to verbalize a need to let go further; this is a normal and necessary preparation for a parent's death.

WHY FAMILIES MUST BE VIGILANT

Somehow families must steer a path between trusting the nursing home and constant vigilance toward it. Some of the horror stories about nursing homes are, unfortunately, true. There are nursing homes that are foul-smelling warehouses for the living dead where old people are left to lie unattended in their own body wastes. You would never put your parent in such a place. But even a good facility can deteriorate. A change in ownership or management takes place, an administration begins to cut corners financially, a staff suffers from burnout—and suddenly, problems begin to show up in the kind of care your parent is getting.

The need for vigilance in placing a parent and monitoring care is underscored by a national survey of 16,000 nursing homes ordered in 1988 by the Health Care Financing Administration, a federal agency. The survey examined the facilities in thirty-two federally rated categories, including quality of patient care, protection of patients' rights, and others. The survey revealed that

▶ 42 percent of those surveyed failed to store, prepare, and distribute food under sanitary conditions;
▶ 30 percent failed to provide residents with adequate

personal hygiene;
▶29 percent failed to properly administer prescription drugs;
▶25 percent failed to insure rehabilitative care to prevent deformity and paralysis;
▶25 percent failed to isolate sick residents to prevent the spread of disease;
▶18 percent failed to take steps to prevent skin deterioration;
▶9 percent misused drugs to control behavior; and
▶2 percent failed to protect residents from mental and physical abuse. (Many nursing home reform groups believe that the last figure is misleading, since abuse is notoriously underreported.)

The law does make certain requirements that nursing homes must live up to, but unless families are vigilant, these laws may not be enforced. (The survey speaks for itself on the subject of enforcement.) You need to know what the law requires. At the same time, you want the kind of loving care for your parent that is almost impossible to legislate.

When Martha moved her mother to a Lutheran nursing home near her brother, she worried about whether she was doing the right thing. But her mother could no longer stay in a board-and-care home, and her name had come up on the waiting list just when she had to move. Martha needn't have worried. The first night her mother (who suffers from dementia and is disoriented) was in the nursing home, she was, naturally, frightened and unable to sleep. Instead of drugging her into unconsciousness, the aides held her all night to comfort her. What legislature would dare to require that?

WHY AREN'T THERE MORE CHRISTIAN NURSING HOMES?

If only there were more nursing homes giving that kind of love! In looking for a nursing home, you might start looking for those run by Christian denominations, only to find that in many parts of the country they're in short supply. I suspect it's because there are so many other pressing needs competing for the churches' attention—drugs, AIDS, the homeless, and daycare for children, to name a few.

However, the need for loving nursing home care is an opportunity for Christian business people to serve the Lord by caring for the sick and frail elderly. You won't get rich doing this, but if you're a skilled manager, you can charge the going rate, pay employees a decent wage, and still earn a profit.

In evaluating nursing homes, don't be fooled by those who use the name "Christian." They can be wolves in sheep's clothing. The owner of an intermediate care home in my county used to tell families, "I'm a Christian. This home is my ministry." He had to sell the business when he was charged with, and pleaded guilty to, raping one of the residents. Another local businessman, a prominent layman in a Protestant denomination, had one successful nursing home but got greedy. He tried to expand rapidly into a chain by buying other facilities but ran into cash flow problems and went bankrupt. He couldn't pay the staff, and his formerly good nursing home deteriorated so much that it lost its Medicare certification.

CHOOSING A NURSING HOME

Most people, when they think of nursing homes, have in mind skilled care facilities. But there are other types of facilities.

The lower level of care is sometimes called "board and care" or "intermediate care." In addition to a room and meals, board-and-care homes provide supervision of medications and help with dressing and bathing. Some also provide help with toileting. Most require that residents be ambulatory, but some will take people who use walkers or wheelchairs. Often, these are "Mom and Pop" types of businesses, with owner-managers living on the premises. They usually provide a more homelike atmosphere than skilled care facilities do, but often there are no planned activities for residents. Only some states license board-and-care homes. Charges range from $500 to $1500 and up monthly. Medicare and Medicaid do not pay for this, since it's considered custodial care. However, some of these facilities take Supplement Security Income (SSI) recipients.

Skilled care facilities provide around-the-clock nursing services. A physician must certify that a patient is sick enough to need these services, and bills are covered by Medicaid for those who meet the income restrictions. Costs for private care are $1800 to $2500 and up monthly, which Medicare does not pay for.

Your parent's physician can help to guide you to the level of care your parent needs, and your local Area Agency on Aging should be able to provide you with lists of licensed facilities in each category.

The first consideration in choosing a nursing home is financial. Since the average annual cost of skilled nursing home care in the United States was $22,000 in 1988, few elderly can afford to pay for private care for very long. When a patient has used up all his assets, Medicaid (Medical in California), a program for indigent and low-income people, takes over. One of the saddest commentaries on aging in the United States is this: You can work hard all your life, save your money to take care of yourself in old age, and still end up indigent and on welfare. If your parent gives away assets in order to qualify for Medicaid, the law requires that this be done thirty months before entering a nursing home. Federal legislation, which took effect on September 30, 1989, permits the spouse of a Medicaid nursing home resident to keep $786 in monthly income and $12,000 or half the couple's assets, whichever is greater. Previously, most states required both partners' assets to be used for nursing home care, making the spouse who was not in a nursing home penniless.

People who qualify for Medicaid are usually also eligible for SSI. A nursing home administrator, a social worker, or your local agency on aging can explain the details to you and tell you how to apply.

Your very first question should be, "Does my parent have enough money to enter a nursing home as a private patient— at least for a while?" If not, he must enter as a Medicaid patient, and you will have to confine your search to nursing homes that accept Medicaid patients. Since most nursing homes prefer private patients (they pay more and there's less governmental red tape), some will not take Medicaid patients at all. This will narrow your choices considerably.

What if your parent enters as a private patient, then uses up all her money and has to go on Medicaid? According to federal law, she must be given thirty days' notice before she must leave.

What to Look for in a Nursing Home

Booklets and checklists are available to help you look for a nursing home for your parents. (See Appendix.) To summarize briefly, your first priority should be the quality of patient care. I've seen beautiful, even luxurious, facilities that were seriously understaffed. Others, less fancy perhaps, put more money into staff salaries and less into interior decorating (which is often done more for the benefit of visitors than residents).

How do you assess the quality of patient care? The key is the staff. High staff morale is important to good care. Most patient care in convalescent hospitals is done by aides, not nurses. You can tell a great deal just by the general atmosphere when you visit. Are the workers cheerful and friendly? Do they call residents by name and treat them with respect? Or are they silent and sullen, overwhelmed by the demands of too many patients?

Do they speak and understand English? In many areas of the country, aides are hired from the ranks of recent immigrants who are willing to take low-paying jobs. Many come from countries where the old are loved and respected, but not all speak English well enough to communicate with old people. The elderly have enough difficulty hearing and understanding without the further hindrance of trying to deal with poor English language skills.

Other key questions to ask include, "How much is the staff paid?" "Are they unionized?" "Are they allowed to work double shifts?" "Who does relief on weekends?" "What is the rate of staff turnover?" "Are aides certified by the state?" "Does the facility train its own staff?" "Does it have in-service training? By whom?" "How many R.N.s on staff?"

In too many nursing homes today, workers, who are often single mothers, are paid minimum wage and need to work double shifts or have two jobs to survive economically. It's not desirable to have an exhausted aide take care of your parent after working an eight-hour shift at another convalescent hospital.

It is a good idea to drop in unexpectedly on a weekend. Sometimes an otherwise well-run hospital becomes chaotic on weekends because the regular staff is off and poorly supervised relief workers from agencies fill in. Try to come at different times of day. Arrive in the morning and observe whether most residents are up and dressed by 10:00 a.m. Are the activities announced on the bulletin board actually going on? Come at noon or other mealtimes and see how the food is served. What is the atmosphere of the dining room? Eat at least one meal there. What is the quality of the food? Visit in the evenings and see if the residents are put to bed too early, for the staff's convenience. Whenever you visit, do you smell any pervasive odor? (Some urine smells are probably unavoidable, but they shouldn't be present constantly.) Sit awhile where you can watch call bells and time how long the staff takes to respond.

Will your parent's doctor be able to come to this facility? If not, who is the doctor on staff? In far too many convalescent hospitals, the staff doctor stands in the doorway of the patient's room and says, "How are you?" The patient says, "Fine," and the doctor bills Medicare for a patient visit. If this is what you're faced with, you'll either have to find a doctor willing to come to the home or take your parent to a doctor outside the facility to get good medical care.

YOUR PARENT'S RIGHTS AS A PATIENT

When your parent enters a nursing home, she (or you, acting on her behalf) will be asked to sign an entrance or admissions agreement, which despite its informal appearance is a written contract. (A sample admissions agreement is printed on pages 263-265 to give you an idea of what to expect.) You need to read this agreement carefully, be sure you understand it, and perhaps, have it read by your attorney.

Provisions of this contract do not supersede state and federal laws. For example, most admissions agreements have statements like, "The facility is not responsible for personal effects such as dentures, glasses, hearing aids, etc." However, California state law now says that the facility is responsible for such effects and spells out in detail what it must do to protect them. Other states may have similar requirements, so families need to familiarize themselves with the state laws regarding nursing homes. Their best source of information is usually the nursing home *ombudsman*.

The ombudsman (a word borrowed from the Norwegian) is a government official in Scandinavian countries who investigates citizens' complaints. In American nursing homes, he or she is usually a volunteer who mediates and negotiates between the nursing home resident and the nursing home administration. Under federal law, each state is required to have a long-term care ombudsman.

In two-thirds of the states, ombudsmen can enter nursing homes and talk to residents and staff. Acting either on their own or on complaints received, they take up problems with the administration. (Patients, who are isolated, vulnerable, and often fearful of retaliation, seldom complain on their own behalf; nine times out of ten, it's the family who complains.) Ombudsmen cannot order a nursing home to take action or shut off the home's federal funds. But they can report violations to the licensing authorities. Often their best weapon is the threat of calling violations to public attention through the media.

If the name and phone number of the ombudsman is not posted inside the nursing home, you should be able to learn who the ombudsman is from your Area Agency on Aging.

Federal legislation passed in 1987 spells out the rights of nursing home patients; a partial summary is given below:

1) To choose a personal physician, be kept informed about care and treatment, and be allowed to participate in planning their own care;
2) To be free from physical or mental abuse and punishment, including involuntary seclusion and physical and chemical restraints (unless needed to ensure safety);
3) To have privacy in accommodations, medical treatment, written and telephone communications, and visits and meetings with family and resident groups;
4) To voice grievances and have them addressed, particularly in resident groups;
5) To remain in the facility and not be discharged or transferred without reason and due process, including thirty days' notice.

The National Citizens Coalition for Nursing Home Reform (see Appendix) can provide the names of local organizations that act as "watchdog" groups on behalf of nursing home patients and their families. One such group, Bay Area Advocates for Nursing Home Reform, based in San Francisco, California, organizes support groups for families of nursing home residents in Bay Area counties and has sponsored legislation against nursing home abuses. But these laws mean nothing unless families are aware of them and insist on compliance.

Lois McKnight, director of the Ombudsman Program in Contra Costa County, California, recommends the formation of family councils in nursing homes. By comparing notes, families can know whether a violation is an isolated incident or part of a pattern. And by banding together, they cannot be dismissed by the administration as "just one chronic complainer."

Through family councils, family members can make new friends and find support for each other in a trying situation. A family member can go away for a weekend or a week's vacation with the assurance that another patient's family will watch out for her loved one while she's gone—and that she'll do the same for them.

Family councils also band together to show appreciation for the staff. One family council gave an ice cream social for the nursing home staff to show their appreciation. (Nobody had ever done anything like that for these workers before!)

In most cases, a great deal can be accomplished by building positive relationships with administrators and staff, but there may be times when you must complain. They are more likely to listen to complaints if you've complimented them in the past on the things they've done right.

When you must complain, follow the chain of command. Speak first to the director of nursing, then to the administrator, and if neither of these people correct the problem, go to the ombudsman. Make your complaint specific—one or two things, not a dozen—and brief. Tell what happened, who it happened to and when and where it occurred. Try to include a statement of what you'd like done about the problem.

If you're not satisfied with the response, seek counsel from someone more knowledgeable about nursing home law, such as the ombudsman or a local advocacy group.

The most common complaints in nursing homes are about the quality of the food, misplaced clothing, rude or careless treatment by staff, unanswered call buttons, and theft of personal items. Poor quality food is inexcusable. The cause is either incompetence or an attempt to cut costs or both, and both are correctable.

Occasional slowness to answer call buttons could mean only that someone on staff called in sick and left the home temporarily shorthanded. However, a continual problem means either understaffing or poor supervision or both. Theft is something the administrator can discourage, if not totally eliminate. For example, are stolen items reported to the police? If not, why not?

Some disappearances are losses rather than thefts. To minimize these losses, patients' families should mark dentures, eyeglasses, and hearing aids with names or initials. It would also be prudent to furnish the administrator with a list of possessions that the patient is taking into the nursing home, with photos, if possible. Clothes should also be marked with name tags, although many families prefer to do the patient's laundry themselves, both to save money and to cut down on the number of misplaced items.

A NEW SET OF CHALLENGES

"I thought when my wife entered a nursing home, I'd have more time. But I haven't done any of the things I thought I'd do. Sometimes, I just sit around the house and cry," said Ned, a Florida caregiver.

Caregivers who place a loved one in a nursing home are exchanging their old problems for a set of new ones. To summarize the challenges: you need to remain vigilant and concerned as your parent's advocate, do what you can to make your parent's life in the nursing home better, and do all this when your own emotions are making it difficult for you to be either energetic or rational.

While there is no way you can change the situation, you can change the way you view it. Instead of a dreaded duty, your visits can become an opportunity to serve the Lord. The entire nursing home (and not just your parent) could become your ministry. Since you'll be spending so much time there anyway, you'll have an opportunity to get to know the staff, the administrators, and the other patients and their families. You can make a difference in that nursing home.

Begin praying for the staff and others you come in contact with. Nursing home aides have difficult, often dirty, jobs with low status and low pay. Sometimes, they're verbally abused by patients. They may have to endure racial slurs. Their chief source of self-esteem in their jobs is the positive response of patients and their families, and families tend to see only what's wrong, never what's right. Perhaps nobody ever praises them or thanks them, but you can. Look for ways to compliment them for a job well done.

In addition to praise, use your creativity to think of other little awards. How about small gifts—flowers or vegetables from your garden, homemade cookies or jams, a message button from the card shop that says, "You're special!" cards, and notes?

Good nursing homes welcome the active participation of patients' families. Some sponsor support groups for families. One of the duties of the administrator should be to counsel and educate families that have had no contact with nursing homes before and don't know what to expect. Sometimes families have unrealistic expectations that may be created by their emotional reactions.

"When I look back on my complaints," said Liz Rummel in an interview, a former caregiver who is now a nursing home administrator, "I can see that they were something to zero in on when I couldn't do anything else. I couldn't feed my mother anymore, but I could find things to complain about. It was a way for me to channel some of my anger and frustration."

What can you realistically expect? In order to help answer that question, I'd like to recommend three books. I've already cited *When Love Gets Tough, the Nursing Home Decision* by Rev. Doug Manning in another chapter. I especially like his chapters on "Adjusting to the Decision" and "Living with the Decision."

You, Your Parent and the Nursing Home, the Family's Guide to Long-Term Care, by Nancy Fox, R.N., is an experienced geriatric nurse's detailed account of what to expect and what you, the patient's family, can do to help your loved one and the nursing home. This book gives a detailed discussion of what to look for in a nursing home, a fuller version of the patient's bill of rights (see page 213), and suggestions for making life in a nursing home "life more abundant."

The third book is a slim one, only twenty-four pages long. It's *Caring Relationships, Guide for Families of Nursing Home Residents* by Hope Cassidy and Linda Flaherty. It has a lot of helpful suggestions and insights packed into a very small space. (See the Appendix for how to order these books.)

WHEN YOUR PARENT IS NEGATIVE

If your parent is negative whenever you visit, you begin to feel like a child who dreads going home from school because she knows she's going to get punished as soon as she gets there.

Sometimes your parent's negativity is a part of the adjustment process. It's caused by anger and grief, which are natural reactions to loss. If you allow your parent to express his emotions, he's more likely to work through them and get over them. This will require all your reflective listening skills (see chapter 3).

If the complaints are about you, it helps if you can learn not to take them personally. Your parent must really feel confident of your love if he can show you this much negative emotion! If the complaints are about the nursing home, you'll have to evaluate whether they're valid or a way of focusing his anger. If the latter, try by reflective listening to get through the surface complaining to the real feelings underneath. Above all, be patient. The adjustment process and working through all these feelings take time.

But what if the negativity and attacks on you continue? Some caregivers have used confrontation successfully by saying, "You know, it's very difficult for me to come and see you when you're always so angry with me." Their parents took the hint and backed off. They needed to have the caregivers set some limits.

Often, "Shall we pray about it?" is the most effective response to negativity. Praying for and with your parent and reading Scripture together can help both of you spiritually. Even the nursing home patient who is too sick to respond in any way can be comforted in his spirit, so don't make your actions dependent on your parent's response. This is also a good time to use the "comfort verses" mentioned in chapter 10. Print one or two in large letters and place it where your parent can see it. Even if he can no longer read because of a stroke or dementia, it will have a positive impact, if not on him, on the staff and others who come into the room.

What can you do to make your parent's experience in the convalescent hospital more positive? Many books recommend fixing up his room with family pictures and personal possessions. For a patient who no longer communicated, her daughter put up a large poster board in her room. On it, she listed her mother's favorite foods, favorite colors, former hobbies and accomplishments, where she was born and grew up, and other personal details. This helped the staff to relate more to her mother as a person.

HOW TO MAKE VISITS MORE ENJOYABLE

Many families dread visiting because conversation is so difficult. Even if the patient is physically able to communicate, you will both run out of things to say. But it's your presence that's important to your parent, not your conversation. You can communicate nonverbally with hugs and pats and smiles. You can sit with her and watch television, if that's what she wants to do, or bring needlework to do. You can offer to write letters for her or send cards to people she'd like to keep in touch with. You can read out loud.

Bring things in that will be stimulating: photos that trigger memories and encourage reminiscing, simple crafts, games to play together, pictures that you change frequently, and music or books on tape. If your parent is still capable of doing so, this would be a good time to tape record memories and put together a book. The game "Generations," mentioned in chapter 3, can be used to draw her out. Another popular noncompetitive game, The Ungame, can be useful in sharing feelings.

Don't forget babies and young children; old people love them and little children can be so loving in return. (But don't force children if they seem fearful.) Are you permitted to bring in pets? These can be a great source of pleasure to nursing home residents.

Is your parent able to be taken out on short outings? Even a trip to McDonald's for a hamburger can be a treat. Shopping is often too exhausting, but you can take her to the mall to "people watch."

What can others contribute? A teenager in one family visited and played his guitar. Church Sunday school classes have "adopted" nursing homes, with each child building a one-to-one relationship with a resident. Does any church group come to visit or conduct services? If not, would her church do so? Would yours? Does her pastor or yours visit? Don't be too shy or too proud to bring this need to others' attention.

Get acquainted with the activities' director, who can always use volunteers. Is there some group activity you can help with that would benefit other residents as well as your parent?

DON'T NEGLECT YOUR OWN NEEDS

During the time that your parent is in a nursing home, you will often find yourself on an emotional roller coaster. You may, for example, be emotionally drained after visiting. This is not the time to neglect your own needs. Review the suggestions in chapter 4 and reach out for help. One caregiver found it helpful to keep a daily log—a kind of journal—in which she wrote about what happened, how her mother was, and what she, herself, was feeling. If writing helps you, write. Others may need to talk to a counselor or find solace in a support group. Whatever it takes to keep going as a caregiver and supporting your parent in the nursing home, do it!

Often, as human beings, we seem able to focus only on the hurt of seeing our parents decline and the guilt of being unable to care for them personally. From that point of view, having a parent in a nursing home is a depressing experience. But if we can look beyond our narrow perceptions, we may see countless examples of love, courage, caring, and faith inside nursing homes.

There is a perception that residents in nursing homes are all miserable. True, many of them are very sick. But even though the lives they're living are quite restricted ones they *are* living, and many of them are glad to be alive. When one activities director asked residents to share what they were thankful for, their responses included "for being," "for my family," "for not being quite broke yet," and "for Jesus." These are people who have something important to teach us all. Let those who have eyes to see, see.

12

Walking Through the Valley of the Shadow of Death

Yea, though I walk through the valley of the shadow of death, I will fear no evil: for thou art with me.
Psalm 23:4, KJV

Familiar words. Beautiful words. How many times in our lives have we heard, read, even prayed the words of Psalm 23 ourselves? Yet until we actually find ourselves experiencing the valley of the shadow of death (whether our own death or a loved one's), we can never fully appreciate this scripture. The psalmist writes, "For thou art with me." No other experience will bring us closer to God, but I don't find many Christians rushing out to embrace the experience of watching a loved one die.

American Christians live in a death-denying culture, shrinking from the subject like any pagan. (If you don't believe me, announce a course on death and dying in your Sunday school and watch the classroom empty out.)

When you're young, it's easier to sustain the illusion of immortality. But when you become a caregiver, you realize that the elderly person you care for is going to die. And after your parents die, there's no getting around the fact that your life is also drawing to a close. You'll be next! What a frightening thought!

And what an opportunity to grow as a child of God. It's not morbid to think about death. This is a great turning point in your life. If you give in to your fears and run away from your parent's death, you will miss whatever God wants you to gain from this experience. But if, instead, you face death and your own fears, you have the promise that God will be with you.

OUR PARENTS' FEARS

In many cases, our parents will be way ahead of us in their attitudes toward death. (God has had more time to work on them!) If they are Christians, they may be looking forward eagerly to the final stage of their life's journey. Or they may believe, yet still be fearful. One of the greatest fears of all is fear of the unknown, and death is the last great unknown. (Even Jesus said, "The spirit indeed is willing, but the flesh is weak" [Matthew 26:41, RSV].)

Death is also the one last thing we can't control. We can try, in our prayers, to specify the manner of our deaths, yet Jesus seems to rebuke Peter for being concerned about how John will die (John 21:20-23), and tells Peter that he (Peter) will be led where he doesn't want to go (John 21:18). Our elderly parents may pray for an easy death—just to go to sleep and not wake up—or they may pray to be taken quickly before they become a burden to their children. These prayers may or may not be answered in the way we wish. It isn't easy to pray "Not as I will, but as thou wilt" (Matthew 26:39, RSV).

Often our elderly parent will not fear death so much as the whole process of dying. Nobody wants to be kept suspended indefinitely between life and death by machinery, to lie in a vegetative state, body bristling with tubes. Such is the fate that modern medicine has decreed for too many unfortunate sufferers. You can't guarantee that this won't happen to your parent, but there are steps that both of you can take to avoid it.

EXPERIENCING A "GOOD DEATH"

If there is a Christian attitude toward death, I believe it's not to escape death (for this is impossible), nor is it to make a quick exit so we can maintain the illusion of controlling our own destiny, but a Christian attitude toward death is to experience a "good death" in accordance with God's will. The Apostle Paul writes, "I have fought the good fight, I have finished the race, I have kept the faith" (2 Timothy 4:7, RSV).

What is a "good death"? I believe a good death, when one has had time to prepare, is one in which a person is ready to leave this earth because he feels his work here is completed. He can move on to the next world without regret because no "unfinished business" is tying him to this one.

In his book *Aging Parents, How to Understand and Help Them*, Dr. Richard P. Johnson, a clinical psychologist, describes some research that found that terminally ill people from dysfunctional families take longer to die.[1] At first Dr.

Johnson was baffled. How could it be that people from healthy families where there was open communication, joy, and love, died sooner than people from unhealthy families? Shouldn't the opposite be true?

Then he understood. People from healthy families know that the family will be able to carry on without them. They are ready and at peace. In contrast to this, people from unhealthy families feel great unease. ("How can they get along without me?" they ask.) They hang onto life grimly, unable to let go and die in peace.

The person who feels that his life has been a disaster—that nothing has gone right—will be terrified of dying. This is the only life he'll have and it's going. There won't be a chance to do it over. Suddenly, death confronts him with all of the issues he's spent a lifetime avoiding. If such a person can come to accept his own life, forgive others for whatever went wrong, and accept forgiveness for himself, he can still experience a "good death." Jesus can be his Savior, as He was to the thief on the cross. He, too, can die in peace.

In some families, one family member can't let go of the dying person even though he may be suffering a great deal. To help a loved one die a "good death," you may have to release him. You may even need to tell your parent in so many words that it's "okay to die."

That will be difficult if you are holding on to some unfinished business with your parent. You may have some emotional work to do before you can release him.

The pioneering modern book on death, *On Death and Dying*, subtitled, *What the Dying Have to Teach Doctors, Nurses, Clergy and Their Own Families*, by Elisabeth Kübler-Ross, M.D., was written after Dr. Kübler-Ross, a psychiatrist, had been asked to participate with four theology students in a research project. As they interviewed patients, she observed how uncomfortable doctors and nurses felt in talking to patients about death and how reluctant they were even to be around the dying. The tendency of the staff to isolate such patients impoverishes the doctors and nurses as well as the patient, Dr. Kübler-Ross believes.

In her book (which is widely used in the training of doctors, nurses, social workers, and some clergymen), Dr. Kübler-Ross formulates five stages that dying patients go through. Families need to be aware of these stages, which do not adhere to a neatly defined progression. It's possible to go back and forth from one to another or to remain "stuck" in one stage for a long time.

1) *Denial.* In the first stage, the dying person denies what is happening to her. She may look for a doctor who will tell her something different. She may believe that the laboratory made a mistake. Denial is healthy when it acts as a buffer to ward off some of the shock that the dying person experiences. Even those who move beyond denial will usually return to it from time to time.

2) *Anger.* In the second stage, the patient asks angrily, "Why me?" She feels angry at God and envious and resentful of the healthy people who will live on. People who have been able to exert a lot of control all their lives frequently react to dying with rage. The patient may have angry feelings that originated early in her life that she has never resolved. Now they come tumbling out. She may take out her anger on family members, doctors, nurses, and others around her. They usually feel quite unfairly attacked, but if they can understand the reason for the anger, they don't have to take it personally.

3) *Bargaining.* In this stage, the patient makes promises to God to "be good" if only He will postpone the inevitable. Often the patient will not reveal her efforts at bargaining with anyone. Sometimes the bargaining reveals some guilt feelings that need to be worked through.

4) *Depression.* Unable to keep up her denial, aware that bargaining won't work, at the fourth stage the patient becomes depressed by the impending loss of everything that is dear to her in this world. Trying to cheer her up is useless and may impede the necessary preparations she must make for her coming death.

5) *Acceptance.* If the patient has been able to work

through the previous stages and talk about her feelings, she may come to the stage of acceptance, which is almost devoid of feelings. Having found peace, she appears detached and no longer interested in what's going on around her. Family and nursing staff who feel she's "giving up too soon" may communicate that she's being cowardly and selfish by not fighting on to the end. This can make her dying a painful experience.

At this final stage, the patient no longer fears dying, but she may fear abandonment. What your loved one needs most at this stage is the reassurance that she will not be left to die alone.

THE CAREGIVER'S EMOTIONAL ROLLER COASTER

When you experience the final illness of a loved one, you, and others around her, will also experience denial and anger. Dr. Kübler-Ross found nurses who denied there were any terminally ill patients on their floor. Doctors became angry at patients who were not getting well. Similarly, you may find that family members will tell themselves that Grandma only needs a little rest and she'll be fine. They may even be angry at you.

How will you handle family members who cling to denial? This is a hard one. It's difficult to talk people out of denial; usually, they come through it when they're ready to. But a family member in denial can make it very difficult to do any necessary planning. You may also find yourself reacting with anger and resentment toward this person.

Anger is a common emotion of the patient's family. As a caregiver, you may find yourself becoming angry at your parent for being so sick, crazy as this may sound. You may become inappropriately angry at doctors and nurses. You may find yourself bargaining. You will certainly become depressed at your coming loss. But with God's grace, you will reach the stage of acceptance and be willing to let your loved one go. If you experience her death as rejection or failure, if you implore her, in the words of the profoundly pagan poem by Dylan

Thomas, "Do not go gentle into that good night. Rage, rage against the dying of the light," you are thinking more about your own needs than you are about hers.

Many people have said (and it was also my experience) that during a long terminal illness, you do most of your mourning before the actual death takes place. You will find yourself on an emotional roller coaster. It's especially difficult when there are "false alarms." Death may be expected, yet the person pulls through. You were prepared for the death, but now you have to start the whole process over again. You wonder how much longer it will take.

Some caregivers may find it difficult to go to church because familiar hymns (especially the parent's favorites) start the tears flowing. Is your church a safe place to cry? (If not, some caregivers find they have to go someplace where they're not known. Some even feel they must stop going to church.) You need to allow yourself to have these feelings and not to choke off or deny them. You'll need a comforting shoulder to cry on, to let all these emotions out. Here's where Christian friends can help, just by listening.

During a crisis, everybody must make a decision either to face the experience and grow, or to run away from it. You may be angered and disappointed by family members who withdraw from your parent because they can't face their own reactions to death. If someone lacks the strength to face death right now, you'll just have to pray that God will grant it to him at some later time. You can't make the decision to grow for him.

Instead of trying to change anybody else, save your energy to do whatever it takes to keep yourself going. For me, it was exercising every day at the health club indoor pool. (Water was appropriate. I often sat in the hot water of the whirlpool with hot tears running down my face. But afterwards I felt better, got out, and kept going.) I also kept a journal sporadically. Many people find in writing a way to let out their emotions. They even communicate better with God in writing.

Most people, including the person who is dying, find it very difficult to talk about death. Should you bring the subject up? Or should you wait for her to bring it up? How sad it would be to pass from this life never talking to those we love about anything but cheerful trivialities! Yet this does happen. We all need to take off our masks.

When to say something is a delicate matter. If you attempt it too soon, when a dying person is in denial or depression, she may rebuff you. If you wait too long, your loved one may be too ill, too weak, or too much under the influence of drugs to communicate. If that happens, you can still fall back on nonverbal communication. Holding her hand, stroking her hair, or if she's in an oxygen tent and you can't touch her, just being there and giving her loving looks are all ways of saying, "I love you. I care about you. You're important to me."

My mother, who didn't like to be touched and found it extremely difficult to express positive emotions, came to the place of acceptance in the hospital just before cancer surgery. Struck down and too weak to struggle anymore, she let me hold her hand by the hour, stroke her hair, and even thanked me for all my husband and I had done for her. She also reassured me, "Whatever happens, it's all right."

Without saying, "I'm dying; good-by" in so many words, she was still saying good-by. This was very precious to me.

MODERN HOSPITALS MAKE DYING HARD TO DO

I've decided to tell my personal story because it's fairly typical of the difficult decisions that families often have to face. Even if you and your parent decide that you will not allow doctors to take any heroic measures to sustain life, circumstances may take some of these decisions out of your hands.

In most acute care hospitals, death is regarded as an affront. Such hospitals exist to make people well. The attitude often seems to be "If someone insists on dying (especially on my shift), we in this hospital have failed. All of our effort must go toward helping those who are going to live, so we have no time to waste on the dying."

"When you enter an acute care hospital, you're asking to have everything done that they possibly can do to keep you alive," says Joyce Terry, R.N., a geriatric nurse educator and consultant for Christian Action Council. This explains the heroic efforts hospitals make to keep people alive at all costs and the tendency of a hospital staff to ignore those who are obviously going to die. I had hoped and prayed that my mother would not have to die in a hospital, but this was not to be.

She began failing visibly shortly before Thanksgiving 1985 at the age of eighty-nine. In February 1986, a sore suddenly erupted on her abdomen, draining blood and pus. She'd had symptoms of stomach problems but had refused x-rays and diagnostic tests because "All they can do is operate, and I won't have any more surgery." She was not in any pain, even from this open sore, but obviously something was very wrong.

Referred to a surgeon by her doctor, I took her to his office for an examination. It was a terrible scene. She loudly insisted she would never consider surgery, and the surgeon (an autocrat who wasn't used to being crossed) angrily told her there was nothing he could do for her if she didn't want to be treated. It was a standoff. I took her home.

A nurse from the county health department came and showed me how to change the bandages on her open sore twice a day. She would check on her once a week, but at that time, that was all the help that Medicare would pay for. I knew I would need help. I was able to hire home health aides who came for part of each day to bathe and dress her and change the bandages.

In March she had a t.i.a. (a short, transient stroke) but recovered and called me into her room, panic in her voice. She couldn't get up from her chair. She struggled and struggled; I tried to lift under her arms, but her legs wouldn't hold her up. I found myself holding her dead weight until I could ease her back into the chair.

I ran to the phone to call the doctor. When I returned, she was gasping for breath with awful, loud, painful breathing. I knelt and put my arms around her. She was so weak that she kept leaning to one side. I tried to prop her up with pillows to see if that would ease her breathing. She began shaking uncontrollably. I hugged her and prayed.

Fortunately, the doctor was in his office only five minutes away and came immediately. By the time he got there, the shivering had stopped but she had a fever of 103 degrees, and her breathing could be heard all over the house.

I called an ambulance and followed it to the hospital in my car. I saw that she was settled in a bed, answered the nurse's questions, then went home and cried. Doug (my husband) came home from work and found me still sobbing. We held each other and cried.

Over the next few days, doctors explained my mother's difficult choices. She could do nothing and continue to die a slow death from cancer, which might take a long time. The open wound would be difficult to manage, and she would have to be moved to a nursing home. I could not take care of her at home in this condition. Or she could have exploratory surgery. This would not save her life, but it offered some hope of making her last days more comfortable. Neither choice was very attractive. Coward that I am, I thanked God that she was mentally capable of making the decision for herself. I wouldn't have wanted to make it for her (yet many caregivers must make similar ones).

After continually refusing surgery, she changed her mind and decided to have it done. When I spoke to the surgeon, he told me the mortality rate for this surgery (death on the operating table) was from 15 to 20 percent for a growth that large. The morbidity rate (death later from complications) was 50 percent. I really felt that in my mother's case the odds were probably much worse. Her lungs were scarred from childhood tuberculosis; even with oxygen, she could hardly breathe. She'd had congestive heart failure for some time and massive doses of Lasix were being given intravenously to get the fluid out of her lungs. I felt she was probably choosing a quick death from surgery over a slow, lingering, painful death in a nursing home.

One of the disadvantages of her choice was the torture of being in a hospital. When she'd refused surgery, the staff did what they had to do but almost ignored her. Now, she was subjected to all the tests, the pokings, the proddings, the blood-drawing.

How little the hospital workers knew about the elderly. One young lab technician said to my mother, "How easily you bruise!"

"Everybody that age bruises easily," I told her.

I sat and watched helplessly while three different nurses tried to start an IV for a blood transfusion. My mother's arms were a mass of bruises.

A young respiratory technician had to give Mom a breathing test before surgery. Mom couldn't blow out one long breath. The technician got exasperated and angry.

"I *am* cooperating," Mom said. "I'd like to see you do it at my age. I'm supposed to be calm before surgery but you people come up here and get me all agitated."

"That's telling her," I thought. But it was so unnecessary. Isn't it possible to train technicians to show compassion for a person whose body doesn't obey her anymore? When you're dying, must you also have people yelling at you?

Surgery was scheduled for 4:00 p.m. My husband and I kept vigil in the second-floor waiting room outside surgery until 10:30 p.m. At last the surgeon came out in his scrubs. The news was, as I expected, bad. The colon was full of cancer, and there was little he could do. He'd resectioned the bowel, but there was still a hole in her stomach where one of the cancers had grown through the abdominal wall. The only comfort I got was that the bowel would soon have become obstructed, necessitating surgery anyway. There really had been little choice.

We went home to a fitful night's sleep. Next day, I was allowed to see Mom in the intensive care unit. She lay on a bed, hooked up to a respirator, with tubes running from every orifice of her body to machinery and IVs connected to bottles. Gowned and masked nurses moved in an almost eerie silence broken only by the hum of machinery and the hissing of the ventilator that was breathing for her.

The news was still not good. Mom's vital signs were not stable and the bleeding hadn't stopped. They were giving her whole blood and platelets. At 6:00 p.m. the surgeon telephoned me at home. He wanted to go back in to see if there was anything he could do to stop the bleeding, but he'd need my permission to operate again.

I put down the phone and started praying for guidance. After praying and talking it over with my husband, I decided to refuse permission. No matter what anyone did, she was going to die. What was the point of putting her through more surgery? The surgeon did not try to pressure me, but I did feel pressure from the nurse in the ICU: "You're not going to allow the surgery?" she asked. "But she's bleeding to death."

The next morning, I was confronted in the waiting room by Dr. X, the cardiologist who had been called in before the operation. He explained to me that my mother's vital signs were now stable. Her heart, lungs, and kidneys were working. The only thing preventing recovery was the bleeding.

"We've gone this far, why not go a little further?" he asked. "Otherwise, she'll bleed to death. It'd be like putting a gun to her head."

I looked into the clear brown eyes of this young doctor in disbelief.

"You're asking me to choose how I want my mother to die—bleed to death now or die later of cancer?" I asked.

"That's right," he said. "I know this is a hard decision."

I was so angry I thought I'd choke. Obviously, he had not a clue as to what a slow death from cancer was like for the patient and the family. I, who had already been through this with my father, knew what my mother and I would face if she survived this surgery. I fought back the impulse to strangle him and said, "If she lives, she may curse me for not letting her die. Have you thought of that?"

He had no answer for that. But this doctor had uner-ringly got through to me by hitting the right guilt button. All of the peace I'd had about my decision left; the phrase, "like putting a gun to her head," kept running through my head. I gave permission for the surgery, which was hastily scheduled for that afternoon.

It did no good. The surgeon found no blood vessels that he could cauterize. He put in packing and platelets and hoped for the best. She stabilized on the table, but soon after her kidneys stopped producing urine. They gave her massive doses of diuretic to get the urine going and dopamine to bring up her blood pressure.

Why are they doing this? I wondered. Apparently, once the wheels of treatment have been set in motion in an acute care hospital, there's no stopping them. But the surgeon had told me she would not be kept alive indefinitely on a respirator. If she couldn't resume breathing on her own, the respirator would, with my permission, be turned off.

I met our pastor in the hospital parking lot; he was there every day to read from the Scripture. She was conscious but not in pain. Her eyes recognized us. I'm sure she was wonder-ing, "Why am I still here?"

On Monday they started trying to wean Mom off the respirator. It was four more days before they let her die. The doctor called—they'd concluded at last that the machine was only prolonging her death. With my permission, which I gave over the phone, they would turn off the machine and give her only oxygen. She died on Good Friday, 1986.

DEATH IN A HOME SETTING

Not everybody has the luxury of choosing where his or her death will take place. But when such choice is possible, many people prefer to die at home rather than in a hospital. My mother's experience illustrates why.

To illustrate the difference, I'd like to contrast my

mother's experience with the death of Helen Hight's mother, who died at home earlier the same year. Helen describes what happened:

"In October, Mom was in pain and in the hospital for a short stay. A vertebra had collapsed. [This fracture was caused by osteoporosis; but she had suffered from arthritis and had been in a wheelchair for years.] The doctor said there was nothing they could do. It might get better and it might not. By Christmas the pain seemed to be subsiding. We had the whole family here [three children and five grandchildren] and she seemed to be doing much better, but she was very tired.

"I had rented a Hoyer lift to get her out of bed [into a wheelchair] because of the pain. But three days after Christmas, she just screamed, 'Put me down,' and I knew something had happened. Her body began to shut down then. She never got out of bed again.

"I didn't know what to expect, but I knew we didn't want to take her back to the hospital. She didn't want to go back. It was too traumatic. And we didn't want her to die in the hospital. But I had a lot of apprehension. I had never been with anyone who died, and I didn't know what it would be like.

"On January 10 my brother and sister-in-law had come down from Oregon. They called on the phone, and I said, 'Things aren't that bad,' but they felt impressed to come. So I called all my kids and asked them to come over that night.

"After dinner, Philip [Helen's oldest son, who has a beautiful voice] sat on her bed with all the grandkids, and I asked, 'Mom, would you like Philip to sing for you?' She nodded yes and squeezed his hand and we all sang some of her favorite hymns.

"After church the next morning, the name of Bonnie Kick, a hospice nurse who belongs to our church, came to my mind. I thought about Mother dying, and I thought, 'I really would like to have her opinion and to have her explain to me what to expect. I called her and she was there in twenty minutes.'

"We went into Mom's room, and Bonnie looked at her

and said, 'She's really close.' Mom wasn't responding at all.

"I told Bonnie, 'I couldn't get her to take her medicine,' and she shook her head at me as if to say, 'Don't bother.' I'd noticed when I got up that morning that Mom was super-cold and very white.

"Bonnie looked at me, a big smile on her face, and said, 'She's very close. I'll just sit here with her while you have dinner.'

"My other brother and sister-in-law [who live nearby] had also come, so we all sat down and ate. After dinner, I went back in Mom's room to talk to Bonnie. She thought Mom was breathing a little more comfortably. I said, 'Now, I want you to tell me what to expect,' and we were standing at the bed talking.

"Bonnie looked down and said, 'She's going now.'

"'You're kidding!' I said.

"'No. She's going.'

"'That easy?' I gasped. 'That simple?'

"And she said, 'She's gone.'

"At first, I was so astonished I didn't know what to do or what to say. I bent over and kissed her. Bonnie walked into the kitchen and told my brothers, 'Would you like to be with your mother? She's just slipped away.'

"I was in awe of what had happened. It was a beautiful experience. If I'd known, I wouldn't have been frightened at all. I've talked to others who've had family members die at home and it was very similar for them."

This, to me, is a beautiful example of the kind of death anyone might hope for. At home, amid familiar surroundings, comforted by familiar scriptures and hymns, surrounded by a loving family—then, as if a door had been opened, slipping through it to be with God. It's a good death not only for the dying person but for the family because it removes all fear and leaves only good memories behind.

Unfortunately, not everybody is able to nurse a parent at home. But with support from outside (such as hospice, described below), many families could do it.

THE HOSPICE IDEA

One of the blessings of a terminal illness spent at home is that it gives the dying person time to reflect on his life, to make peace, to ask forgiveness if necessary, and to say good-by to loved ones. This is impossible if he's in intractable pain or if his mind is clouded by pain medication. Hospice, by supporting families who care for the dying at home and controlling their pain, has allowed many to experience a "good death."

Hospice is an Old French word from which we derive the modern word *hospital*. It meant a shelter or lodging for travelers, children, or the destitute, often maintained by monks.

Sandol Stoddard writes in *The Hospice Movement*, "In Medieval times, dying persons were seen as prophetic souls, voyagers and pilgrims valuable to the community in a number of ways, not least in the opportunity they provided those around them for service and spiritual growth. It is a modern and ignorant prejudice to consider death a failure. It is a modern superstition to avoid knowledge of it, to treat it as if it were something unnatural, shameful or wrong."[2]

The modern hospice movement began in the 1960s in England under the leadership of Dr. Cicely Saunders, a Christian M.D., and reached the United States about a decade later. By 1986 there were about 1700 hospice programs nationwide. In England, hospices are actual buildings, places where dying patients go when they can no longer be maintained at home. In the United States, separate hospice buildings are rare (although some hospitals do maintain hospice units). Hospice is most often a system of home care, supported by a team of doctors, nurses, health aides, social workers, and volunteers. It differs from ordinary home care in that the family, not just the patient, is the unit of care.

To receive hospice services, patients, families, and doctors must agree that the patient is terminally ill with six months or less to live. After admission, the hospice team, consisting of doctors, nurses, chaplains, and in some hospices, social workers and psychologists, cares for the family's needs around the clock, seven days a week. Trained volunteers provide respite care for the family and counseling through the bereavement period. Medicare and some private health insurance policies now pay for hospice services.

The Importance of Pain Control

Dr. Saunders demonstrated, early in the hospice movement, that patients can be maintained virtually free of pain, able to enjoy life and to interact normally with family and friends. Although they receive enormous amounts of pain medication, they do not become zombies or drug addicts. Unfortunately, the American medical establishment has been very slow to accept this finding.

Pain management is one of the greatest gifts that hospice gives to a dying patient's family. It is also the most convincing rebuttal to the "humanitarian" argument of the euthanasia proponents. They say terminally ill patients must be allowed to choose suicide to escape the pain. This is not true. Ninety-six percent of terminally ill patients can be free of pain; the remaining four percent can be made more comfortable.

My authority for that statement is Robert J. Brindley, Pharm.D., oncology (cancer) pharmacist coordinator at the John Muir Medical Center in Walnut Creek, California, for fourteen years, and pharmacist for Hospice of Contra Costa for ten years.

The drug most used in pain management is morphine, administered orally. If necessary, Dilaudid (a trade name for hydromorphone), which is five times more potent than morphine, can be given. These drugs have been shown to be as effective as heroin (which was the drug first used in English hospices), so that there is no reason to press for the legalization of heroin. However, these drugs are not effective alone for some types of pain (e.g., bone pain) for which aspirinlike analgesics are used.

In addition to choosing the right medication, you must administer it correctly. Enough has to be given on a regular basis. If you wait until the pain becomes unbearable, you set up a fear/anxiety pain cycle that worsens the pain and is one of the causes of tolerance and addiction. Dosages must be adjusted to the individual. If he becomes drowsy or oversedated, the dosage must be lowered until he is alert but pain-free.

"We need to listen to the patient," Dr. Brindley said. "He's the expert on his pain. I once asked a patient what she needed from us [the medical team]. At first she said, 'I need compassion.' Then she stopped herself and said, 'I need *competent* compassion.'

"The medical community is not that skillful in pain management. One of our jobs is to let them know that the fears they have about strong narcotics are invalid," Dr. Brindley said. "I've worked with over 1,000 cancer patients and not one has become addicted. If they get better and their pain goes away, we can cut the dosage and even eliminate the narcotic altogether, and there's no problem of withdrawal. As long as you're taking the medicine for pain and taking it appropriately, you don't get addicted."

What if you think your parent's doctor is not managing his pain well? Talk to the physician, Dr. Brindley advises. He may be totally unaware of what's going on. Tell him what you need. Or ask a nurse who is working with your parent to speak to the doctor.

The doctor may have prescribed pain medication that your parent isn't taking because of fear of addiction. In this case, the doctor or a nurse who's conversant with pain management needs to talk to your parent to allay his fears.

Hospice and Spiritual Needs

Each hospice is different, so the description Bonnie Kick, R.N., a nurse with Hospice of Contra Costa, gives of a hospice nurse will not apply universally. The hospice she works for is a private one, supported entirely by contributions; it's been in existence for ten years.

"Our nurses act as case managers," Bonnie said. "I visit my patients at least once a week, meeting with them and the

family, assessing their needs. We bring in community resources wherever necessary, possibly contacting the family's
church if that hasn't been done to see if there's something they
can do to give the caregiver a break. I encourage the caregiver.
Usually, they think they're not doing enough when they're
doing a super job. I teach nursing skills, little tricks that make
the job easier.

"If there's pain when they're first admitted to hospice, we
jump on that right away, trying to adjust the medications or
getting them to take the medicine the doctor prescribed. But
not all pain is physical—the pain can be coming from spiritual concerns. We have a lady like that now. She's a committed
Christian, but she thinks Christians 'aren't supposed' to have
pain, be angry, and so forth. Some of her anxieties are coming
from [the belief that] 'I'm not supposed to feel this way
because I'm a Christian.' Our chaplain has been very effective
in working with her.

"In general, though, the nurse is the one who's not afraid
to let the patients talk about what their concerns really are.
We try to be good listeners, let them lead the conversation and
talk about whatever seems to be bothering them."

Every person near death has spiritual concerns and needs
to have these concerns addressed. The hospice movement so
far has been very cognizant of patients' spiritual needs. What
an opportunity this provides for Christian nurses and volunteers. Bonnie prays for her patients and with them, if they
wish. She lets them lead the way, staying sensitive to what the
Holy Spirit is doing in a person's life at this particular time.

This is not easy work. I don't know how it's possible
without a deep faith in God. And, in fact, hospices are very
concerned about burnout among nurses and volunteers.

"You can't work with dying patients effectively if you're
not secure with your own mortality," Bonnie says. "You have
to accept death as a part of life before you can help somebody
else."

Hospice workers don't view death as a failure. Their
reward is not only a good death for the patient but seeing

families coming together and getting closer and stronger. Because of this, Bonnie says that this is the most rewarding nursing she's ever done.

Hospice is not for everyone. It tends to be limited to cancer patients, since with most other diseases it's more difficult to predict when death is imminent. Even with cancer patients, it's sometimes difficult to know when hospice becomes appropriate. Some doctors still resist the concept and will not refer patients. Some families may feel that their privacy is violated by the team approach or fear revealing problems in their family relationships to total strangers. Also, family members must be strong enough not to panic and cause a crisis. If your loved one is taken to an acute care hospital, he will be put on life support, which is what you are trying to avoid.

Hospice and Euthanasia

Hospice, by ending dying patients' pain, ended the euthanasia movement in England. But in the United States, the euthanasia movement has been making rapid progress while most Christians have looked the other way. Publicly, the various euthanasia societies promote "the right to die," which sounds harmless enough. But as their own internal literature makes clear, what they really want is the legalization of assisted suicide. I am not talking about "letting people die" by withholding extraordinary life support when there is no hope. I'm talking about measures such as an attempt that failed in 1987 to get an initiative on the ballot in California that would have allowed physicians to give lethal injections on demand.

The pro-euthanasia forces include the Society for the Right to Die (formerly the Euthanasia Society of America), Concern for Dying, the Hemlock Society, and others. At the 1984 International Conference of the Societies for the Right to Die, a four-step agenda was announced. First was the social and legal acceptance of living wills, then suicide and assisted suicide, euthanasia, and finally suicide clinics, similar to abortion clinics.

Instead of promoting the "right to die" (which will soon become, if I'm not mistaken, the "duty to die"), we could attempt to find solutions to some of the causes of suffering among the elderly and their families. As a nation, we could reduce medical costs, emphasize the prevention of chronic illness, and strengthen families that are struggling with the care of elderly relatives.

There is no denying that much needless suffering is caused by medical technology. Norma is the younger sister of my best friend, Clare, from college days. Their mother is terminally ill with a neuromuscular disease (similar to Lou Gehrig's disease). For years, she's been in a hospital in New York City, bedridden, unable to swallow, unable to speak, tube-fed, and breathing with the aid of a respirator. Norma, the family caregiver, visits once a week, traveling three hours round trip to do so.

Norma wrote to me: "I am filled with sadness for her and for myself. I had no choice in the matter of placing Mother since nursing homes do not accept respirator patients. I am angry at the brother who won't share the burden. [Her two sisters live on the West Coast.] I am resentful. I ask, 'Why me?' and I answer myself, 'Why not me?' I am weary and pray that mother will die—now—and yet I feel she'll live a long time so there's no end to it. I will be so relieved when she dies. I am furious at the medical profession who play God and keep her alive. And I guess I'm angry at her for staying alive. Please pray for me."

This is tragic, and I can certainly understand why Norma is angry at the doctors. They placed her mother on the respirator without asking anyone, including her. I asked my friend Clare if going on a respirator had been her mother's decision.

"My mother never made a decision in her life!" Clare said, "First, her father told her what to do, then her husband. Whatever a doctor said, she did."

It's hard to refuse a respirator and choose to die. Yet it's equally hard to believe that Norma's mother would have agreed to be put on a respirator if she'd known the kind of slow, lingering death she was choosing. Perhaps she didn't know. Perhaps it was never explained to her. Most hospitals do this without consulting loved ones. After hospitals turn the respirator on, most states require a court order to get it turned off.

ETHICAL AND MORAL DILEMMAS

The living will, which is legal in thirty-eight states and the District of Columbia, has been promoted by euthanasia groups as the answer to this dilemma. (A living will form is reproduced on pages 267-268.) As you can see, the language is somewhat vague (i.e., How do you know whether a procedure will prolong dying?). But it's extremely difficult for a living will to cover every possible situation. Do you want your mother to give instructions never to be put on a respirator? But what if your mother were in an auto accident, was put on a respirator for support, recovered and lived another ten years? How can you be sure that hospital personnel will respect a living will? You can't. If your parent is brought to an emergency room in respiratory distress, she's not going to be in any condition to tell the e.r. personnel, "I have a living will. Don't put me on a respirator." Medical personnel are trained to act quickly in emergencies, not to debate the chances for recovery. There are few cut-and-dried situations. Even with a living will, doctors will go to the family to make a final decision.

Under common law, everyone has the right to refuse medical treatment. However, it's sometimes very difficult to exercise this right. Doctors, nurses, and hospitals often pressure patients and their families to accept treatment. Patients also fear being abandoned by their doctors if they refuse the recommended treatment.

Hospitals and nursing homes, fearing lawsuits, may demand written evidence, such as a living will, that a person unable to speak for herself would not have wanted the treatment. If your parent is unable to make choices, you will have to do so, and you may have to be prepared to prove that your choice is what your parent would have wanted.

Euthanasia forces have confused the issue by introducing the term "passive euthanasia." Refusing treatment and allowing a dying patient to die is not "passive euthanasia," and nobody should be made to feel guilty for making this choice for a parent.

A new instrument, the durable power of attorney for health care, is now legal in a few states. This gives a third party (usually a family member) sweeping powers to make health care decisions for another if she becomes unable to make them for herself. Under California law, a durable power of attorney for health care can be given to someone who will be the beneficiary of the patient's estate. The potential for abuse is obvious, and unlike guardianship, the decisions of the person holding durable power of attorney for health care are not subject to review by a court.

Whether there is a living will or a durable power of attorney for health care, your parent's doctor is going to approach her family for decisions anyway. So families need to try to be prepared.

The best protection against the horror of medically prolonged dying is an understanding in advance with the doctor who's caring for your parent. If your parent is mentally competent, she should discuss with her doctor what she would or would not want done. She should ask the doctor to explain in some detail what will happen if she refuses a respirator or refuses food or fluids. And she should let her family know what she's decided. Becoming informed and communicating openly are the best protections your parent can give herself and you against the abuses of overly-aggressive treatment.

If your parent is not mentally competent, you should have this conversation with your parent's doctor. During a crisis situation, it's difficult to think clearly. You may have to make a quick decision before you have time to mull things over and to pray about it.

If the doctor is not comfortable with your parent's wishes on death and dying, it's best to find this out sooner rather than later. You don't need a doctor who, to bolster his ego or assuage his fears, tries by every means possible to prevent his patients from dying when their time comes.

MAKING FUNERAL ARRANGEMENTS

Many seniors, in the course of "putting their house in order" (chapter 7), make advance arrangements for their own funerals. This is not morbid. It's a wonderfully loving act that relieves families of making burdensome decisions when they're under emotional stress and find it difficult to think clearly. But if this has not been done, it becomes part of the work that needs to be done by the elder and his family during terminal illness.

Your pastor can guide you, especially if he knows your parent, about the services. For other details, a guidebook that tells you what you need to do is listed in the Appendix. It's best to make your plans and talk to funeral directors before you're in shock or grief.

CHRISTIANS ALSO NEED TO GRIEVE

The Apostle Paul, writing to the Thessalonians, said, "But we would not have you ignorant, brethren, concerning those who are asleep, that you may not grieve as others do who have no hope" (1 Thessalonians 4:13, RSV).

Many Christians have taken this passage to mean that Christians have no cause to grieve. But it doesn't say that. It says they do not grieve the same way as those who have no hope of the resurrection.

You often hear Christians say to their friends and family, "I don't want any weeping and wailing when I'm gone. I want you to rejoice and celebrate because I've gone to be with the Lord." This is a well-meaning attempt to spare loved ones pain, but it isn't scriptural and it doesn't work. Jesus wept when Lazarus died, and so did Mary and Martha. Nobody said, "Cheer up! He's gone to a better place."

Until you've done the hard work of mourning, you are not yet out of the valley of the shadow of death. And you can't run away from it; you can't get out of it except by going through it.

Some years ago, a lady of strong faith in our church lost her husband after nursing him through a long illness. She believed Christians should rejoice when one of their number has gone to be with the Lord. No tears for her! Smiling happily, determined to make her experience a witness for her Lord, she spoke at her husband's memorial service, preaching a beautiful sermon on her husband's life and the meaning of death for a Christian. Everybody marveled at her composure. After that, she threw herself into a round of activities. She was out every night at a different class or meeting.

You guessed it. Within a matter of weeks, she collapsed physically, emotionally, and spiritually. She could fool other people, she could even fool herself, but she could not fool her own body, mind, and spirit, and she certainly couldn't fool God, who made us creatures who need to mourn. She thought Christians could be spared the pain of the mourning process and go directly to acceptance. Her behavior also contained a strong element of pride — "I'll show them how a real Christian does it!"

But real Christians go through the same emotions and stages of mourning as everybody else. The difference is the four little words "Thou art with me."

STAGES OF THE MOURNING PROCESS

Entire books have been written about grief and mourning. In this brief space, it's impossible to give more than a sketchy outline of what to expect.

Shock
The chief feeling is numbness. This is a natural protection against being overwhelmed by the full force of your feelings. Shock seems to be more prevalent and longer-lasting when death is sudden and unexpected. Caregivers who have

watched a parent failing for a long time may pass through this stage quickly, or not at all.

Pining
Accompanied by feelings of guilt and anger. Everything reminds the mourner of the lost loved one. He makes himself feel guilty by asking, "Why didn't I do this?" or "If only I'd done that." He may be angry at the loved one for dying and angry at God for taking him. If there was no opportunity to say good-by or to resolve some of his feelings about the dead person, this stage may be prolonged.

Depression
Feelings of hopelessness, lack of energy, and difficulty in sleeping or eating mark this stage of mourning. Counselors recommend against trying to distract the grieving person or taking her to a doctor who will prescribe mood-altering drugs until at least six months after the death. Depression is a normal stage and trying to short-circuit it may delay recovery.

Recovery
In the final stage, the bereaved person's interests in living and energy begin to revive. He's able to get on with his life. He doesn't "forget," but the memories are no longer so painful.

These stages are not a neat progression. Grieving people will move back and forth from one to another. Months later, well into recovery, they may experience flashbacks in which the earlier, painful emotions come flooding back in all their intensity. But they become fewer in number with the passage of time.

GRIEF IS A COMPLEX PROCESS

Some people seem to think that their major feeling—after the prolonged illness and eventual death of a loved one—will be relief. Of course, relief is there, as well as guilt for feeling relief. But our emotions are much more complex than that.

A journal I kept for a while after my mother died is invaluable now in reminding me of that. A lot of what I felt surprised me. The emptiness of the house, for example. (My mother had lived with us for eight years.) One day I wrote, "I feel like a little child whose Mommy has gone away and left her alone in the house."

I found myself having trouble concentrating and wandering around wondering what to do next. I decided not to demand too much of myself and just let myself "float" for a while. Following a death there are plenty of practical things that need to be done, such as paying bills, giving away clothing and belongings, and settling an estate. Take your time and don't push yourself; when you're ready, you will do all these things. And don't hesitate to ask for help if you need it.

One of your last tasks as a caregiver is mourning. God gave us tears for a reason, and this is certainly one of the reasons. Most of us have trouble allowing ourselves to cry in public—it's just not socially acceptable in our culture. But cry you must; you need to get your feelings out in order to recover. Ask God to help you find someone who'll give you a listening ear and a shoulder to cry on. Resolve to be that kind of person later on for someone else in mourning who needs you.

NOTES: 1. Richard P. Johnson, Ph.D., *Aging Parents, How to Understand and Help Them* (Liguori, MO: Liguori Publications, 1987), page 90.
2. Sandol Stoddard, *The Hospice Movement, A Better Way of Caring for the Dying* (New York: Vintage Books, 1978), page xvi.

Afterword to the Reader

When it comes to aging, the "sandwich generation" is in a very different position from its parents. The older generation did not know it would live so long; ours does. They could be excused for not making plans to be old. But we have no excuse for not planning.

With the passing of your parents, your life's journey will enter its final phase, a phase that could encompass twenty or thirty years, or up to one-third of your life. What will you do with this gift of time? What does God expect of you? What does the Bible have to say?

WALKING TOWARD THE LIGHT

The writer of Proverbs wrote, "The road the righteous travel is like the sunrise, getting brighter and brighter until daylight has come" (Proverbs 4:18, TEV). If we have successfully passed through the stage of caregiving for our parents, we are now walking toward the light. What does this mean?

Many of us began caregiving while controlled by outside forces—either parents or circumstances or others' expectations. As we progress, we succeed in freeing ourselves more and more from external controls and learn to turn over more and more control to God. We are no longer the same persons.

How can the caregiving experience change a person?

I thought about this question a lot during my own caregiving days. How would what I was learning about being old affect my own old age? When I was writing this book, I asked every caregiver I interviewed these same questions Here are some of their replies:

▶ "I want to be the very best old person I can be so I can be a role model for my children and the younger people around me." This is a new goal for many people who, before they started caring for an elderly parent, may not have given a thought to what kind of an older person they would become.

▶ "I've learned to be a more compassionate person." Caregiving has given many people a deeper compassion for all suffering, especially the suffering of the elderly. As they stand by elderly parents and are willing to suffer with them, caregivers allow God to work a transformation in their lives. The Apostle Paul put it succinctly when he wrote, "Suffering produces endurance, and endurance produces character, and character produces hope, and hope does not disappoint us" (Romans 5:3-5, RSV).

▶ "I've lost some of my smug self-righteousness. I used to think that anyone who put a parent in a nursing home was awful! When I had to do it myself, I stopped being so judgmental."

▶ "I've learned to take one day at a time. You simply can't prepare for every eventuality, and you can't predict what's going to happen." The experience of caregiving tends to strip caregivers of pride, self-sufficiency and self-righteousness. They learn to have more trust in God or they sink like a stone under the burden.

▶ "I've learned acceptance and to let go of the little things that aren't really that important. I've learned that in spite of everything, life is good!"

▶ "I've learned that I'd better become a more loving person so that others will want to be around me when I'm old!" Older people do not become models of love as part of the natural process of aging. Experts say that as you age, you become whatever you were before, only more so. All of your life, you build the self that will be old. If God was the builder, He will continue to do His work in you—to make you more loving and more like

His Son. If He has not been the builder of your life, it's never too late to let Him take over.

▶ "I've learned that I must take responsibility for my own health and well-being, that it's not selfish to take care of myself." When caregivers see what taking care of a sick elderly person can do to a family, they begin to realize that taking care of themselves is the kindest thing they can do for others. If we can avoid becoming a physical burden, then it's our responsibility to do so.

As a result of what we've learned about the health problems of aging, many of us have gained a new appreciation of how future diseases can be prevented by the choices we make now. Exercising, controlling what we eat, not smoking, avoiding or cutting down on alcohol, and above all, keeping our thought processes positive ("Whatsoever things are pure . . . think on these things" [Philippians 4:8, KJV]) — all these things will make us healthier older people. It would help if churches would take a more active leadership role in guiding members to make the right health choices.

Churches could also encourage older members to interact with the young and do more to bring the generations together. Former caregivers, who have learned the importance of intergenerational relations, could also make themselves more available to the church family as they age.

Your experience and wisdom are too precious to be wasted. As God gives you the grace to become a more loving older person, resolve to share some of that love with younger members of your church.

▶ "I'll never put my children through this!" I've heard a lot of caregivers say this. Remaining totally independent all one's life may not be an achievable goal. Nobody knows what disabilities the future may bring. It's impossible to guarantee that our children will never have to take care of us. But we can take steps to lighten their load.

As a loving older person you can put your financial affairs in order, make practical choices about where to live before change is forced on you, communicate your wishes about death and dying, make funeral arrangements, and talk to your adult children about your feelings.

Of course, your adult children may not want to hear you. But talking to your children about these matters may open up communications on a deeper level than you've ever had before. It's worth trying—over and over, if necessary.

A TIME FOR HEALING

"To those who have strained relationships with their families, I'd say, 'Patch things up before you get to the caregiving stage' or it's really going to be rough." If you have "unfinished business" with any members of your family, now is the time to attend to this before illness, disability, or death makes it impossible. The healing of broken and strained family relationships is probably the greatest work you can do at this stage of your life.

Not all of the responsibility for a relationship is on one side. But perhaps pride is preventing you from asking forgiveness or from making the first gesture. If this is your situation, then pray that God will give you the strength to speak and leave the results to Him.

The greatest gift we can give our adult children, and the one thing that will benefit us most in our old age, is to set them free. Often we are not aware of all the unconscious ways we try to keep them under our control. Ask God to open your eyes to what you've been doing. If you've been withholding your blessing from one or more of your adult children, give it at once. It will return to bless you in your old age.

RELATIONSHIPS WITH GRANDCHILDREN

If you've been blessed with grandchildren, caregiving may have given you a new appreciation for the grandparent-grandchild relationship. If your parent had a poor relationship with your children, I'm sure that this made your caregiving task that much harder. Now is the time to form the bonds with your children's children that will hold later when the going gets rough.

This isn't always easy. Often we live at great distances from our grandchildren. (Although, if you have not yet retired, caregiving may influence whether you decide to move to a retirement home far from your family.) Sometimes divorce breaks or loosens family ties. It takes a great deal more time, energy, and ingenuity nowadays to have a relationship with grandchildren. But it's worth working at.

Sometimes we have a tendency to feel that communication is the children's and grandchildren's responsibility. When they fail to approach us, it's tempting to throw up our hands and withdraw. But we are supposed to be older and wiser; we can enter their worlds more easily than they can enter ours, if we make the effort.

If you have never shared who you are with your children and grandchildren, you may want to write your autobiography, tape your recollections and family stories, and get the family photo album in order. Even if your family doesn't appreciate this now, they will later. Don't wait until it's too late.

WORK OUT YOUR OWN SALVATION

Old age is hard work! The experiences of the last stage of life lend new meaning to the words of the Apostle Paul, "Work out your own salvation with fear and trembling, for it is God who works in you to will and to act according to his good purpose" (Philippians 2:12-13). This has always seemed so paradoxical—if God is at work, why do I have to work, too? But I've learned from caregiving that it's only when I take the responsibility for acting on God's promises and step out in faith—even if it's only the tiniest step on the path He's marked out for me—that He really begins to work in my life. That's the great adventure that will not end until we draw our final breath.

Appendix

CHAPTER ONE: THE CRUCIBLE OF CARING

CAPsule, monthly newsletter. Children of Aging Parents, 2761 Trenton Rd., Levittown, PA 19056. Yearly membership fee of $15.00.

"A Checklist of Concerns/Resources for Caregivers," leaflet. AARP, 1909 K St. NW, Washington, DC 20049. Single copy free.

Coop Networker, newsletter. Family Practice Center, St. John's Mercy Medical Center, 615 S. New Ballas Rd., St. Louis, MO 63141. Free.

Horne, Jo. *Caregiving, Helping an Aging Loved One.* Des Plaines, IL: AARP/Scott, Foresman and Co., 1985, $13.95 (paper).

Norris, Jane. *Daughters of the Elderly: Building Partnerships in Caregiving.* Indianapolis, IN: U. of Indiana Press, 1988, $12.95 (paper).

Parent Care, bi-monthly newsletter. U. of Kansas, Gerontology Center, 315 Strong Hall, Lawrence, KS 66045, $20.00 per year.

Silverstone, Barbara, and Helen Kandel Hyman. *You and Your Aging Parent.* New York: Pantheon Books, 1982, $8.95 (paper).

CHAPTER TWO: YOU CAN'T "FIX" OLD AGE

Episcopal Society for Ministry on Aging, ed. *Affirmative Aging.* Minneapolis, MN: Winston Press, 1985, $9.50 (paper).

Johnson, Richard P., Ph.D. *Aging Parents, How to Understand and Help Them.* Liguori Publications, One Liguori Drive, Liguori, MO 63057, $3.50 (paper).

Koch, Kenneth. *I Never Told Anybody: Teaching Poetry Writing in a Nursing Home.* New York: Random House. A moving account of how the author, a well-known poet, taught elderly nursing home residents who had never written before to create poetry. A testimonial to the possibilities for human growth at the last stages of life.

Tournier, Paul. *Learn to Grow Old.* New York: Harper & Row, 1975.

CHAPTER THREE: THE SKILLS OF ACTIVE LOVING

"Generations" game. Generations, Inc., P.O. Box 41069, St. Louis, MO 63141, $24.00.

Schlintz, Victoria, R.N. "How to Communicate with Those Who Hurt." 3241 Colusa St., Pinole, CA 94564. This course could serve as a model for churches everywhere.

CHAPTER SEVEN: LOVE AND MONEY

Essential Guide to Wills, Estates, Trusts and Death Taxes. AARP/Scott, Foresman and Co., 1865 Miner St., Des Plaines, IL 60016, $12.95.

"Estates: Planning Ahead," pamphlet. Northern California Cancer Program, 1301 Shoreway Rd., Ste. 425, Belmont, CA 94002.

"Medicare Handbook," "Medicare Has Improved: Catastrophic Protection and Other New Benefits," and "Guide to Health Insurance for People with Medicare." Published by the U.S. government's Health Care Financing Administration. Consumer Information Center, P.O. Box 100, Pueblo, CO 81002. Single copy free.

CHAPTER EIGHT: WHERE TO FIND HELP

ABLEDATA. National Rehabilitation Information Center's database lists over 15,000 commercially available products that help disabled individuals live more comfortably at home. Call weekdays between 9:00 a.m. and 5:00 p.m.

EST, 800-34-NARIC. Or write NARIC, 4407 Eighth St., Washington, DC 20017.

"All About Home Care: A Consumer's Guide," pamphlet. National HomeCaring Council, 235 Park Ave., New York, NY 10003, $1.00.

American Society on Aging. Dennis R. LaBuda, ed. *The Gadget Book: Ingenious Devices for Easier Living.* AARP/ Scott, Foresman and Co., 1865 Miner St., Des Plaines, IL 60016, $10.95 (paper). The book contains a list of hundreds of items that will help keep your parent independent, with lists of manufacturers and distributors. (See chapter 8 for examples.)

Care manager networks include: Senior Care Network, Huntington Memorial Hospital, 837 Fair Oaks Ave., Pasadena, CA 91105; American Aging Network Services, 80 University Pl., Ste. 4, New York, NY 10003; and Private Practice Geriatric Care Managers, 111 E. 85th St., New York, NY 10028.

Catalogs of helpful products are free from Homebound Resources, Ltd., P.O. Box 180082, Austin, TX 78718-0082; Cleo, Inc., 3957 Magfield Rd., Cleveland, OH 44121; and Independent Living Aids, Inc., 1500 New Horizons Blvd., Amityville, NY 11701.

Christian Action Council, 701 W. Broad St., Ste. 405, Falls Church, VA 22046.

Directory of Geriatric Care Managers and Support Groups for Caregivers. Children of Aging Parents, 2761 Trenton Rd., Levittown, PA 19056, $10.00.

Do It Yourself Listening and Signaling Devices for People with Hearing Impairment. Order this and a list of other helpful devices for people with a hearing impairment from Fellendorf Associates, 1300 Ruppert Rd., Silver Spring, MD 20903, $4.00 (paperback). Fellendorf Associates also has a list of demonstration centers where people with hearing problems can see and test various assistive devices.

Easter Seal Society. Your local chapter provides many services for disabled people, including help with the purchase of equipment for low-income families.

"Handbook About Care in the Home." AARP, 1909 K St. NW, Washington, DC 20049. Single copy free.

"Home-Made Money," publication on home equity conversions, and "Miles Away and Still Caring," pamphlet. AARP Fulfillment, P.O. Box 2240, Long Beach, CA 90801, free.

Lighthouse for the Blind has more than 200 low-vision centers. There are also local offices of the American Foundation for the Blind. You can take your parent to one of these to receive assistance in adapting to failing vision. Your local Lions Club may also be able to help.

National Association of Care Managers, Box 6920, Yorkville Finance Station, New York, NY 10128.

National Federation of Interfaith Volunteer Caregivers, 105 Mary's Ave., P.O. Box 1939, Kingston, NY 12401.

Robert Wood Johnson Foundation, P.O. Box 2316, Princeton, NJ 08543-2316.

Shared Housing Resource Center, 6344 Green St., Philadelphia, PA 19144.

Spargo Pierskala, Carol, Ph.D., and Jane Dewey Heald, M.S. "Help for Families of the Aging" (an eight-week seminar). Support Source, 420 Rutgers Ave., Swarthmore, PA 19081.

Talking Books are a free service of the Library of Congress. Inquire at your local public library.

CHAPTER NINE: WHERE CAN YOUR PARENT LIVE?

"Consumer Guide to Life-Care Communities," pamphlet. National Consumer League, 1522 K St. NW, Ste. 406, Washington, DC 20006, $3.00.

Kraus, Anneta S., R.N. A Guide to Supportive Living Arrangements for Older Adults. Geriatric Planning Services, 116 W. Possum Hollow Rd., Wallingford, PA 19086.

"National Continuing Care Directory," profiles more than 365 life-care communities in thirty-nine states. AARP/

Scott, Foresman and Co., 1865 Miner St., Des Plaines, IL 60016, $19.95.

Shared Housing Resource Center, 6344 Green St., Philadelphia, PA 19144.

CHAPTER TEN: COPING WITH THE HEALTH PROBLEMS OF AGING

Alzheimer's Disease and Related Disorders Association, Inc., 70 E. Lake St., Chicago, IL 60601; or call 800-621-0379.

American Cancer Society, 3340 Peachtree Rd. NE, Atlanta, GA 30305.

American Parkinson's Disease Association, 116 John St., New York, NY 10038.

"Arthritis: Basic Facts" and "Self Care for Osteoarthritis and Rheumatoid Arthritis." Arthritis Foundation, 1314 Spring St. NW, Atlanta, GA 30309.

Blodgett, Harriet, Evelyn Deno, and Virginia Hathaway. *For the Caregivers: Caring for Patients with Brain Loss.* Metropolitan Council, 300 Metro Square Bldg., 7th and Robert St., St. Paul, MN 55101.

Community Care Project, U. of Illinois School of Social Work. *A Handbook of Practical Care for the Frail Elderly,* 1986. Oryx Press, 2214 N. Central, Phoenix, AZ 85004-1483.

Coping and Caring: Living with Alzheimer's Disease, booklet. AARP, 1909 K St., NW, Washington, DC 20049, free.

"Family Survival Handbook: A Guide to the Financial, Legal and Social Problems of Brain-Damaged Adults," pamphlet. Family Survival Project, 1736 Divisadero St., San Francisco, CA 94115.

Graedon, Joe and Teresa. *50 + : The Graedons' People's Pharmacy for Older Adults.* New York: Bantam, $13.95 (paper).

"Help Yourself to Better Breathing," "Chronic Bronchitis," "Emphysema—Answers to Your Questions." American Lung Association, 1740 Broadway, New York, NY 10019.

How to Talk to Your Doctor, pamphlet, and "Maintaining

Continence: Bladder Control in Older People." UCLA/ USC Long Term Care Gerontology Center at UCLA Medical Center, 10833 LeConte Ave., Los Angeles, CA 90024, $1.50.

Incontinence. For more information, send a self-addressed, stamped, legal-sized envelope to The Simon Foundation, P.O. Box 815, Wilmette, IL 60091; or Help for Incontinent People, P.O. Box 544, Union, SD 29379.

Mace, Nancy. *The 36-Hour Day: A Family Guide to Caring for Persons with Alzheimer's Disease, Related Dementia Illnesses and Memory Loss in Later Life*. Baltimore, MD: Johns Hopkins U. Press.

National Parkinson's Disease Foundation, 1501 NW 9th Ave., Miami, FL 33136.

Prescription Drug Handbook. AARP/Scott, Foresman and Co., 1865 Miner St., Des Plaines, IL 60016, $13.95 (paper).

"Seniors: Diabetes and You" and "The 'Other' Diabetes." American Diabetes Association, 1660 Duke St., Alexandria, VA 33214.

"Strokes: A Guide for the Family," "Aphasia," "Heart Facts," and "Stroke: Why Do They Behave that Way?" American Heart Assn., 7320 Greenville Ave., Dallas, TX 75231.

"Using Your Medicines Wisely: A Guide for the Elderly," pamphlet published by the U.S. Public Health Service Alcohol Drug Abuse Administration. Single copy free from AARP, 1909 K St. NW, Washington, DC 20049.

CHAPTER ELEVEN: WHEN YOUR PARENT MUST BE
IN A NURSING HOME

Cassidy, Hope, and Linda Flaherty. *Caring Relationships, Guide for Families of Nursing Home Residents*, 1982. Augsburg Publishing House, 426 S. Fifth St., Minneapolis, MN 55415 (pamphlet).

Fox, Nancy. *You, Your Parent and the Nursing Home*, 1984. Geriatric Press, P.O. Box 7291, Bend, OR 97708.

How to Select a Nursing Home. U.S. Dept. of Health and

Human Services, Health Care Financing Administration. Order from Consumer Information Center, P.O. Box 100, Pueblo, CO 81002.

Kraus, Anneta S., R.N. *Guide to Supportive Living Arrangements for Older Citizens*, 1984. Geriatric Planning Services, 116 W. Possum Hollow Rd., Wallingford, PA 19086.

Manning, Doug. *When Love Gets Tough, the Nursing Home Decision*, 1983. Insight Books, Inc., Drawer 2058, Hereford, TX 79045.

National Citizens Coalition for Nursing Home Reform, 1825 Connecticut Ave. NW, Ste. 147B, Washington, DC 20009.

"Nursing Home Life: A Guide for Residents and Families," pamphlet. AARP, 1909 K St. NW, Washington, DC 20049.

"The Right Place at the Right Time: A Guide to Long-Term Care Choices," pamphlet. AARP, 1909 K St. NW, Washington, DC 20049. Single copy free.

CHAPTER TWELVE: WALKING THROUGH THE VALLEY OF THE SHADOW OF DEATH

Coleman, Barbara. *A Consumer Guide to Hospice Care*. National Consumer's League,

International Anti-Euthanasia Task Force, U. of Steubenville, Steubenville, OH 43952.

Kübler-Ross, Elisabeth. *On Death and Dying*. New York: Collier Books, 1969, $4.95 (paper).

Nelson, Thomas C. *It's Your Choice: The Practical Guide to Planning a Funeral*. AARP/Scott, Foresman and Co., 1865 Miner St., Des Plaines, IL 60016, 1983 (paper).

Stoddard, Sandol. *The Hospice Movement: A Better Way of Caring for the Dying*. Vintage, 1978, $4.95 (paper).

AFTERWORD TO THE READER

Meeting Health Needs Through the Church, pamphlet. Self-published by Victoria Schlintz, R.N., 3241 Colusa St.,

Pinole, CA 94564, $2.00.

Walnut Creek Presbyterian Church, 1720 Oakland Blvd., P.O. Box 5606, Walnut Creek, CA 94596, has published two leaflets to sensitize people to the needs of the ill and their families. "My Mom's Sick, Here's How to Help" by Wendy Bergren; and "Through Affliction, God Teaches Me" by Carole Danzig. (Single copies, $1.00 each.)

TO THE READER: Do you have any comments or suggestions about caregiving? Any experiences you'd like to share? Are there any helpful resources you've used? Please send them to

Barbara Deane
321 Lake Meadow Ct.
Martinez, CA 94553

_____ Convalescent Hospital

Admissions Agreement

In consideration of _____

_____ , patient, being admitted to our Hospital as a patient, the undersigned jointly and severally promise and agree as follows:

ADVANCE DEPOSITS

An advance deposit of $_____ shall be made upon admission, receipt of which is hereby acknowledged. Within thirty (30) days after discharge, the advance deposit will be refunded after deducting charges accrued to date of discharge. Once each year we offset all advance deposits against accrued charges as of the last day of our annual accounting period and then bill for new advance deposits on the first day of the new accounting period.

CHARGES

Commencing on the first day of the month following admission and on the first day of each and every month thereafter, the undersigned shall be charged for the following services rendered in the month preceding the billing date:

1. Room, board, and general nursing care at the rate $_____ per day for the actual number of days of care rendered.
2. Drugs, special supplies, laboratory services, physical therapy services, and other services deemed necessary and proper for the health and comfort of the patient.
3. A special linen and laundry charge of $1.00 per day on those days only on which a patient is incontinent.
4. A charge of 50 cents per meal for those meals during which a patient must be hand fed by our nursing personnel.
5. Our daily rate is based on this Hospital rendering long-term care to patients. Should a patient be discharged before the end of his first thirty (30) days, our daily rate for nursing care will be increased by 10% for the number of days stayed, provided that the total charge for nursing service will not exceed the amount of your advance deposit.

PROMPT PAYMENT

Bills are payable within ten (10) days after receipt. Failure to make payment when due shall automatically increase our rate for nursing service by 10% for all unpaid days of care rendered. If an account must be referred to a third party for collection, patient or responsible relative agrees to pay reasonable attorney's fees and/or cost of collection.

REMOVAL AND DISCHARGE

1. Hospital requires a 48-hour notice of discharge and/or transfer given to the nurse in charge, the Nursing Director or Administrator. Patient or responsible relative will be charged a premium two times the daily rate if no notification is given.
2. Hospital reserves the right to terminate service to a patient by giving five (5) days written notice.
3. Discharge time is 11:30 a.m. Patients staying beyond this time will be billed for an additional day.

GOVERNMENTAL PROGRAMS

All services reimbursable through a governmental program are rendered subject to the eligibility of the patient and the acceptance of billings by the fiscal intermediary for the governmental program. The undersigned shall be responsible for all nursing and ancillary charges incurred if eligibility is rejected for any reason by the governmental agency or fiscal intermediary involved.

A patient transferring from one governmental program to another or from the status of a private payment to a governmental program must notify the Hospital in writing prior to change of status. Retroactive eligibility for a governmental program is not recognized by the Hospital. Eligibility commences on the date patient and/or relative delivers to hospital written authorization from the governmental agency involved.

PHYSICIAN REQUIRED

The personal physician of patient is Dr. _____
_____ who may be called to attend the patient by the Hospital in its sole discretion and charged to the undersigned. If the personal physician is not available, the Hospital may call in another physician for patient with such services being charged to the undersigned.

STANDARD HOME EQUIPMENT

Hospital furnishes standard equipment, for the use of patients. If the attending physician orders special equipment (which includes wheelchairs, walkers, etc.) it shall be supplied at extra charge, paid for by the undersigned. Any patient bringing special equipment for personal use does so at his own responsibility, after first obtaining the consent of the Hospital, and a written order by the doctor.

RESTRICTIONS AND LIABILITIES

No foodstuffs, liquors, medicines, or treatments shall be supplied to patient without first obtaining written permission from Hospital. Hospital shall not be responsible for any money, valuables, or personal effects brought to Hospital by patient, relatives, or friends, unless delivered to Hospital's custody for safekeeping and a receipt issued.

Hospital shall incur no liability for injuries of any kind to patient while under its care, except where the injury is caused by the negligence of the Hospital or its employees. Removal of the patient from the Hospital either temporarily or permanently shall terminate responsibility of Hospital.

Hospital reserves the right to move a patient from one bed to another or from one room to another.

The undersigned has read the foregoing and understands the terms and conditions therein.

Dated _____

CMAP NO. _____ Patient _____

    Patient Liability _____ (Other) _____

MEDICARE NO. _____ Street _____

    Hospital Ins. _____ City _____

    Medical Ins. _____ Phone _____

    Termination Date _____ Relationship _____

Admitted by

Living Will

DECLARATION

Declaration made this _____ day of _____ 19 _____

I, _____, being of sound mind, willfully and voluntarily make known my desires that my dying shall not be artificially prolonged under the circumstances set forth below, and do declare:

If at any time I should have an incurable injury, disease, or illness certified to be a terminal condition by two (2) physicians who have personally examined me, one of whom shall be my attending physician, and the physicians have determined that my death will occur whether or not life-sustaining procedures are utilized and where the application of life-sustaining procedures would serve only to artificially prolong the dying process, I direct that such procedures be withheld or withdrawn, and that I be permitted to die naturally with only the administration of medication or the performance of any medical procedure deemed necessary to provide me with comfort, care, or to alleviate pain.

In the absence of my ability to give directions regarding the use of such life-sustaining procedures, it is my intention that this declaration shall be honored by my family and physician(s) as the final expression of my legal right to refuse medical or surgical treatment and accept the consequences from such refusal.

I understand the full import of this declaration and I am emotionally and mentally competent to make this declaration.

Signed _____

Address _____

I believe the declarant to be of sound mind. I did not sign the declarant's signature above for or at the direction of the declarant. I am at least eighteen years of age and am not related to the declarant by blood or marriage, entitled to any portion of the estate of the declarant according to the laws of intestate succession of the _____ or under any will of the declarant or codicil thereto, or directly financially responsible for declarant's medical care. I am not the declarant's attending physician, an employee of the attending physician, or an employee of the health facility in which the declarant is a patient.

Witness _____

Address _____

Witness _____

Address _____

Before me, the undersigned authority, on this _____ day
of _____, 19 _____, personally appeared
_____, _____, and
_____, known to me to be the Declarant and the
witnesses, respectively, whose names are signed to the foregoing instrument, and who, in the presence of each other, did subscribe their names to
the attached Declaration (Living Will) on this date, and that said Declarant
at the time of execution of said Declaration was over the age of eighteen
(18) years and of sound mind.

[Seal]
My commission expires:

_____ Notary Public

This sample form is from A *Matter of Choice*, prepared for the U.S. Senate
Special Committee on Aging. Check requirements of individual state
statutes.

Index

DATE DUE
